Writing Life

Writing Life:
Reflections by West Indian Writers

EDITED BY
MERVYN MORRIS AND CAROLYN ALLEN

Ian Randle Publishers
Kingston ● *Miami*

First published in Jamaica, 2007 by
Ian Randle Publishers
11 Cunningham Avenue
P.O. Box 686
Kingston 6.
www.ianrandlepublishers.com

National Library of Jamaica Cataloguing in Publication Data

Writing life : reflections by West Indian writers /
edited by Mervyn Morris and Carolyn Allen

   p.; cm.

Papers presented at the Mona Academic Conference
2006

   ISBN 978-976-637-329-0 (pbk)

1. Authors, West Indian   2. Creativity in literature
3. Literature - History and criticism
I. Morris, Mervyn II. Allen, Carolyn III. Mona Academic Conference (2006 :
Kingston, Jamaica)

801.92   dc 22

Cover and book design by Ian Randle Publishers
Printed and bound in the United States of America

Table of Contents

Introduction

The annual University of the West Indies Mona Academic Conference is now firmly established as a forum for deliberation and exchange of ideas about issues affecting Caribbean development. Themes that have been addressed include governance, health, labour, gender, higher education and tourism. The 2006 conference — Friday to Sunday, August 25–27 — focused on creativity. Though our creative writers, like other workers in the arts, help us to appreciate the textured reality of our lives, to discover and affirm the people that we are and envision what we can become, our societies have not always understood what writers do and the particular challenges they confront.

We are grateful to our former principal, Professor Kenneth Hall, for having approved the conference proposal, and to his successor, Professor Elsa Leo-Rhynie, for having seen it through. The idea was to bring together a number of writers who would reflect on West Indian life and their experience as writers. The gathering would not be either a festival of readings or a conference dedicated to literary criticism. It would facilitate dialogue among writers, academics and policy-makers, and perhaps increase public awareness of the university's contribution to Caribbean culture.

Writing Life offered a platform to a number of artists, each of whom has been a student or member of staff at the University of the West Indies. There are of course many more writers we would have liked to invite. What the planning committee sought to achieve was a slate that might include various kinds of excellence and might seem reasonably representative of the region's range. Within constraints of time and budget, we tried to be inclusive — in terms of genre, aesthetic assumptions, age, territory of origin, gender and other variables. And though the programme understandably provoked the charge, we did not intend to suggest an invidious distinction between the writers who performed and those who delivered papers. Each presentation represents reflection and a writer's labour in the shaping. We are grateful that most of the writers scheduled for the 'Performance Nights' agreed to be included here.

The order in which the items appear is designed to emphasize connections and contrasts. Self-scrutiny recurs: a careful — often sensuous — probing of the writer's relation to history, community, audience, development, politics, place. Some pieces represent traumatic experiences. Some are inherently theatrical. Some give texture to origins, identity, language, responsibility and so on.

Responsibility, Derek Walcott said on Sunday afternoon, 'has to do with when you discover in yourself that pitch of voice which is not hidden by pomposity, by being away, by looking at your own life and the life of others around you with any kind of veil or any kind of barrier of acceptance or recognition.' He read 'The Schooner *Flight*' and engaged in lively dialogue with the audience.

Feedback suggests that the conference was widely appreciated. If you attended, we hope you will be glad to have the book. And if you didn't, you can catch up now with some of what you missed.

WRITING LIFE
Reflections by West Indian Writers
August 25-27, 2007

August 25

Opening Ceremony

August 26

Session 1 (Chaired by Ralph Thompson)
Olive Senior
Kendel Hippolyte
Merle Hodge

Session 2 (Chaired by Velma Pollard)
Mark McWatt
Kevin Baldeosingh
Jean D'Costa

Lunchtime Readings *by Michael Reckord, Andrew Stone, Kim Robinson Walcott, Tanya Shirley and Andrew Kei Miller*

New Books *presented by Carolyn Allen, Michael Bucknor and Mervyn Morris*

Session 3 (Chaired by Anthea Morrison)
Cecil Gray
Kwame Dawes

Performance Session (Chaired by Karl Williams)
Joan Andrea Hutchinson
The Mighty Chalkdust
Paul Keens-Douglas

August 27

Session 4 (Chaired by Carolyn Cooper)
Erna Brodber
Merle Collins
Honor Ford-Smith

Session 5 (Chaired by Michael Bucknor)
Rawle Gibbons
Jean Small
Alwin Bully

Lunchtime Readings by Paulette Ramsay, Earl McKenzie, Niki Johnson and Marlon James

Session 6 (Chaired by Edward Baugh)
Derek Walcott

Performance Session (Chaired by Jennifer 'Jenny Jenny' Small)
Staceyann Chin
Amina Blackwood Meeks
Brother Resistance

Loving Guyana's Rivers

MARK MCWATT

As I thought about this keynote address I decided not to try to talk about the relationship between my life and my writing (anyway, the things I thought of saying seemed trite and obvious), but to let that relationship become clear by focusing on a part of my life — my childhood and adolescence (when I had the privilege of getting to know the interior of Guyana, especially its rivers) — that I always think of as having given birth to everything I've written and to the sensibility that made it necessary and urgent to write, without ever fully understanding why — the reason for this need. Anyway, I call this piece 'Loving Guyana's Rivers'.

My earliest memories are of crossing the major rivers of Guyana — the Demerara, Berbice and Essequibo — in colonial days on proper ferries: large white vessels, probably made on the Clyde, that always worked and were on time and that had three different classes for passengers and (in those days) could carry only a few vehicles. I suppose it was those early crossings, when I was held at all times and sat on the knees of mother or father on polished wooden benches, that first formed my concept of 'river' and the association that it has since had in my mind with 'excitement' and 'adventure'. It was in Guyana's North-West District, however, that I first became 'intimate' with rivers, the names of which I still love to pronounce, to have them cast their spell again, arousing memories of a total surrender to the seduction of sun and living water: swimming in them, travelling upon them — experiences that for me are still charged with a real physical — almost sexual — pleasure.

From the morning I first arrived at Morawhanna on the Barima River at age seven I knew I would always be hopelessly in love with rivers. The overnight coastal steamer (at that time the S.S. *Tarpon*) arrived and tied up at Morawhanna stelling shortly after dawn and the air was a little chill and I watched the sun burn off the morning mist on the river, and felt it leap into my eyes, reflected from the surface of that wonderful stretch of living, black water. The river also, I was to discover, had a special smell, a strong musk that I found thrilling. We had to get into a small boat with an outboard engine (an Archimedes 10/12) to cross the river to Barima Landing in order to travel by road to Mabaruma, where my father was beginning a tour of duty as a Government District Officer. The bow of the little open boat pushed up high mounds of water on either side as it sped across the river and left a creamy wake behind, and the vibration from the wooden seat and the smell of the river mingled with gasoline and oil from the bilge conspired to create a heady sensual experience for a seven-year-old, and this combination of smells can still summon today every lucid detail of that first trip and others that followed.

I learnt to swim in the rivers of the North West: when I could just about manage to stay afloat, my brothers and I (mostly I) used to pester my father on Saturday afternoons after work to take us to the river to swim. We would fool around in the muddy shallows at Barima Landing and he would stand at the end of the jetty and look out on the big river. One Saturday I went out on the jetty to ask him something and, without answering, he picked me up and threw me into the deep river. I was astonished and broke the surface spluttering and apprehensive. I looked up at him and gasped: 'What to do now, Dad?' and he replied: 'Swim, dammit! You always ask to come here to swim and all you do is splash around in the mud like a crab'. So he directed me: 'Hold on to that pile . . . now push off and swim to this one . . . now swim out into the river a little way and when I shout, turn back.' From then on I would joyfully jump off jetties and wharves all over the country and enjoy the embrace of the river-water and the tug of tide or current . . . and that wonderful smell of the secret life of the river.

I got to know more of the rivers of the North West because my father sometimes had to serve as travelling magistrate and hold court at various small towns and locations on the rivers, and if any of this travel was during the school holidays he would take me with him. We would travel in the District Commissioner's launch (the *Arawak*), which was an enclosed vessel powered by a Lister Blackstone marine diesel. I remember one trip to Arakaka on the upper Barima river. It took three days to get there, overnighting at Red Hill, opposite the ruined sawmill of Mt Everard, and at Koriabo. At first I hadn't wanted to go because I was ten years old by then and attending school in Georgetown, where I had recently acquired a passion for cricket. It was the summer of 1957 and the West Indies were playing in England and I dreaded not being able to listen to the matches. My father surprised me with a special wooden box built to contain a large green radio that worked off huge batteries, stored in separate compartments of the box. The box would be lifted onto the roof (the 'tent' we called it) of the launch and we would sit up there listening to the commentary, which was punctuated by the beat of the diesel engine which the radio somehow picked up — perhaps through the long wire strung as antenna from bow to stern. In the evenings I would bathe in the river and we would sleep in hammocks slung in schoolrooms, draped with very fine nets to keep out mosquitoes and sandflies. On that trip I saw for the first time one evening a family of capybara — the world's largest rodent — bathing in the river shallows near the far bank.

When we reached Arakaka I was supposed to amuse myself while Dad was in court hearing the accumulated cases prosecuted by Sergeant Elcock, who had also travelled from Mabaruma. I realized later that Arakaka in those days was like a Wild West frontier town, because of the influx of (mostly male) workers for the manganese mining that had begun in nearby Matthew's Ridge. I spent lots of time on the river, swimming or in corrials, but I also had cricket on the radio and books to read. One day, in quest of new experience, I wandered into a building and found myself in an adjoining room to the one where court was in session. I heard my father's voice and found a gap in the planked wall through which I could peep at the proceedings. Dad was sitting on a dais surrounded by tables and chairs, and a loud and strapping woman was being charged, apparently, with 'disturbing the peace', because she had started a fight — pulled out a knife and threatened a young man. She was one of the town prostitutes doing a thriving business with the mine-workers. I remember my shock when I heard her assert loudly: 'I ent mind him calling me a whore, but he call me a *fucking* whore, and I can't put up with that kind of disrespect . . . I sorry I ent ketch him with the knife and cut him up good.' Far greater, however, was my shock at what happened next. I saw a completely new and astonishing side to my father and I squinted at the scene in wonder as I heard him say:

'I don't know about you, Sergeant, but I'm having some difficulty with this argument: she doesn't mind being called a whore, but objects to being called a fucking whore. Now I have always understood that it is the business of a whore — to fuck; isn't that so, Sergeant?'

'Yes, Sir.'

'And in fact a whore who does not fuck — apart from being unable to make a living — would be a contradiction in terms?'

I thought I could see Sergeant Elcock's moustache quiver briefly before he put on the most serious of faces and said: 'Yes indeed, Sir.'

In the end the woman was fined forty dollars, but you can imagine the state I was in: it had never occurred to me that my father *knew* those words, let alone that he would utter them in public. That very evening, when I went down to the river to bathe, I was a little frightened to find that the woman and her cronies were themselves in the water bathing. I didn't want to turn back, as they were looking at me, so I slowly eased myself in and heard one say: 'Is Mr McWatt li'l boy; look, he goin' be handsome like he father,' and the woman responded, 'I ent know if the father handsome, but he mout' nasty!' I felt a strange excitement then, as if the river contained and reconciled everything, my unease dissipated and I treasured these little snippets of adult conversation and experience that I sensed would come my way from now on.

On the way back to Mabaruma I listened in agony as the West Indies collapsed in the final test at the Oval and lost the series. Not even Sobers nor Collie Smith could stand up and make runs. I remember distinctly Laker bowling to Collie Smith and the commentator saying 'and he pops that one up into the air and oh, he's caught by May at mid-on', at which point I retreated into the noisy interior of the launch and consoled myself with the thought that England might take away my pride in West Indies cricket, but nobody could ever take from me the constantly unfolding wonder of the Barima river as we rounded each bend, every new reach presenting something fresh and awesome. I affirmed then with a ten-year-old's ferocity born of disappointment, my undying devotion to these rivers and forests and told myself that they would always, always, always belong to me.

There was another such memorable trip, this time on the Waini river, near the mouth of which, on the first morning, my father shot three wississi ducks as they flew up from a patch of reeds and we had curried duck for days. In the lower reaches of the Waini river there are wide lagoons and I always felt that this was a more 'serious' river, whereas the Barima was friendlier and with a great meandering sense of humour. I loved the rest house at Baramanni and every time we spent a night there I would look through the big guest book at all the names of land and forestry officers and other government officials and visitors who had passed through, spending the night in the middle of nowhere. Many of my published poems are about these rivers and the experiences associated with them. Further up the Waini there was the sawmill and the little settlement at Barama Mouth, where I first met Comrade Morgan (I forget his first name), a forestry officer, prodigious rum-drinker and rabid communist who thought that I was good material (at twelve years old) for conversion to the cause — if not to the lifestyle (my father didn't mind me talking to him, but I was not to drink any rum). It was from Morgan that I first heard about the 'bourgeoisie' and 'surplus value'.

One more memory about the Waini river about three years later: by then my father had been transferred to Bartica on the Essequibo, but I refused to break up my relationship with the North West and its rivers just because of that. I was a scout in my Georgetown high school troop and I used to organize camping trips to Hosororo, on the Aruka river: groups of ten to fifteen of us would 'camp' in the school or in tents in the schoolyard and spend our time swimming in the river, hiking to Kumaka or Mabaruma, raiding the fruit trees and bathing in Hosororo falls in the evening.

We heard, this one time, that a boat-load of young people from Hosororo were going to catch crabs at Waini mouth, and some of us managed to get ourselves invited on the trip. Apart from my well-known love for the rivers, there were two important features of this trip: the first was that we all loved to eat crabs, especially the big blue 'bundaree' crabs we were going to look for; and the other was that there was a lovely half-Amerindian girl whom I adored from afar, who was also going on the trip. For me it was heavenly. I actually sat next to Linda and even managed to say a few words to her from time to time as the outboard engine droned on and we made our way down the Aruka, down the Barima, through the Mora Passage and along the left (southern) bank of the Waini towards Punta Playa, the northernmost point of Guyana. The estuary of the Waini is vast and empty and magical and as we made our way towards the mangroves on the river bank, the boat ground to a halt about three hundred yards away for the tide was out and there was this vast mud-flat all around us, covered by scarcely an inch of brackish water. We got out and tried walking towards the trees, but with each step we sank up to the knees into the softest, warmest and purest mud you can imagine: it was slow progress and hard work — until we saw one of the Amerindian boys lie on his belly, push off with his feet and skate twenty yards in a few seconds. All the boys soon followed suit. Try it if you ever get the chance: it's best on your bare chest and stomach (probably best of all completely naked): you just lie on the mud and push off with your feet. The mud is almost frictionless and you speed over it with ease. I can also report that, as a teenager with frenzied hormones who had just sat for hours beside a beautiful girl he longed to touch, it was a very 'arousing' experience as well — lying on the warm slippery mud was what I imagined lying on a warm slippery body would be like, and I was at just the right age to make the most of that. In the end the crabs (of which we caught several quakes — August is crab season), the trip on the river and even Linda herself, take second place in my memory to that wonderful sensation of skating, almost naked, over the warm mud, making sweet love to a river and a continent.

There is also the mystery of creeks, like Wauna and Warapoka: to the uninitiated their entrances are invisible along the seamless vegetation on the river banks, until the experienced steersman suddenly points the bow towards the trees and at the last moment you see the narrowest inlet at an acute angle to the river, and when the boat enters it opens up into a green world of towering trees, diminished light, darting birds and large blue morpho butterflies fluttering ahead of the boat. You have to travel slowly in creeks because of the narrowness and the sharp bends: in larger boats the bowman has to pull the bow around the sharper bends with a giant paddle and to signal to the captain to slow or cut the engine — when, for example, there is a corrial full of children on their way to school, or when a large tree has fallen across the waterway. Often the creek widens at villages into a large and pleasant pool of dark water, with sandy bottom and people bathing and corrials pulled half out of the water. Amerindian corrials (hollowed out forest trees cured and shaped in fire) are the best craft in which to travel the creeks and smaller rivers of Guyana. There are only inches of freeboard and in them you feel very close to the river and to its intimate sighs and whispers, which you can never hear above the noise of engines. Graceful, sturdy and easy to paddle and steer (once you have learned to balance in it), the corrial is a timeless craft, a link to the inscrutable past of these rivers, a guardian of secret creeks and inlets and a comfort for the future, in that whenever all the engines stop and turn to rust, the corrial's magical presence and movement means that the rivers and their remote settlements will still live.

I remember steering a corrial with four of us campers one moonless night from Kumaka stelling to Hosororo: the darkness was profound, except directly above the river, where I knew that the lesser darkness was the sky, my only point of reference. The sounds of the paddle strokes, the little gurglings of the river among the stilted roots of the riverside vegetation and the cries of night-birds and other creatures seemed strangely amplified and not without an edge of fearfulness. None of us spoke much until the lights of the houses and sawmill of Hosororo came into view as we rounded a bend. Then we all spoke loudly with relief, but what *I* felt was an extraordinary closeness to the river itself, as though I had rested my head on its soft, cool belly and listened to all the intestinal noises while it breathed on my neck like a lover. . . . Much as I was excited by engines (the outboards common in those days — like Archimedes and Seagull and the flashier Johnsons and Evinrudes, and also the Lister, Kelvin and Volvo Penta marine diesels that powered the launches and speed-boats of my youth), nothing can match the special feeling I have for the ageless corrial.

Since those North West days, I have come to know many other of Guyana's rivers: the mighty Essequibo, the Mazaruni, the Potaro, the Ireng — and none has disappointed in its power to thrill my senses and produce new wonders: great waterfalls and smaller cataracts and rapids, ruins of ancient Dutch forts, large islands, paradisal beaches like Saxacali and even man-made wonders like the suspension bridge over Garraway stream. . . Things have changed over time: today, on most of the rivers of Guyana it seems that all of the smaller boats are powered by the giant Yamaha engines, from 80 to over 200 horsepower which turn the river and the riverbank scenery into a dancing blur and you focus simply on time and destination. These days there are also 'jet boats', which travel at over fifty miles per hour, and the major rivers are crossed by large Government car ferries and pontoons (when these are actually working!). It is not the same and yet it is exactly the same: the romance of the rivers endures. If you still have a spirit of adventure and wonder and you get close enough to one of the rivers, then its colour and taste and touch and smell cannot fail to tug at your heart. And if you board a Bartica-bound speedboat at Parika with your partner and it begins to rain, you can touch intimately and unnoticed beneath the plastic or leatherette sheets provided for shelter: an experience that will demonstrate what I have always known: that the rivers of Guyana are really for — and about — love.

Fiction as Hypothesis

Erna Brodber

'[T]he insights of the imagination are essential in the developmental process', said the concept paper which invited us to participate. The annual Mona Academic Conference, the concept paper also said, 'has established itself as a forum for discussion of development issues and Caribbean public policy'.

My paper, 'Fiction as Hypothesis', will try to share the way in which 'the insights of [my] imagination' bear on my involvement with 'development issues and Caribbean public policy'. Perhaps I should say it the other way around: how my interest in 'development issues and Caribbean public policy' has led to my involvement with the writing of works of the imagination, for I did not undertake what has led me to be a part of this conference by any determination to be a writer of fiction, but rather by the determination to be a good sociologist whose insights and consequent research could be of use to those trying to include the descendants of Africans enslaved in the New World, into valued spaces in the societies to which their forefathers were brought and in which they have chosen to stay.

Jamaica has been the society with which I have chosen to work. In this work, I have used the exercise of writing fiction to help me to ask the right questions of the sociological field, to formulate hypotheses to guide my social research efforts.

My first major involvement with 'development issues and Caribbean public policy' was the study of abandonment of children in Jamaica, a project to which I was assigned as a research assistant in the department of sociology at the University of the West Indies, in 1968. The findings were published in 1974. My exposure to life in Jamaica through this project led me to the hypothesis that there is a disconnect between those of us charged with the management of development and those of us whom social and economic programmes want to change. If this disconnect does indeed exist, state-sponsored programmes, it follows, are in danger of missing their mark. My first extended work of the imagination, *Jane and Louisa Will Soon Come Home*, was my effort to build a model of this 1970s disconnect in the Jamaican society, to help me to identify the possible elements in this hypothesized disconnect, to identify categories of actors in this disconnect, and to conceptualize the elements that would bridge this breach. I describe the model in more detail below as Hypothesis 1:

> ...that the pre-Independence education system has produced an intelligentsia which is trained to (and does) separate itself from, and consequently disparages, the so-called masses. Such an attitude produces tensions and misunderstanding which themselves make social unity and good governance elusive and retards the amelioration process.

> ...that this position can be reversed if planners were made to examine their family histories and thus made to acknowledge/appreciate their origins and thus see themselves as a part of the whole, no more or less than the others but entrusted with the specialist task of intellectual action which expresses our being.

My effort to use *Jane and Louisa* as a conceptual model for further sociological work on the disconnect in Jamaica society is most easily seen in pages 46 to 51, and pages 78 to 80. Here are the earlier pages.

> My young man's got the spirit. He's turned over a new leaf. He's even changed his profession. He is going to get more learning so that he can better minister to his people. My young man loves his people. He gives half of his salary to his people. My young man talks in an unknown

tongue . . . words like 'underdevelopment', 'Marx', 'cultural pluralism'. I love my young man. He's got the black spirit and it's riding him hard. . . .

25, 5th street houses a government yard. The term government yard denotes a set of ten rectangular rooms joined together. Each room is of the same exact size as the other and has the same exact fittings. Directly behind these rooms is a set of ten smaller rooms, rectangular too but smaller than the above. These rooms too are joined laterally and carry the same exact fittings in each: a water closet marked 5th street, reg. no. 35, a toilet, a shower, and a tiny wash basin.

A little further away is a large cooking area. Why this section is not divided into ten cubicles, to complete the pattern, is the architect's private secret.

25, 5th street has a gate with a tiny porter's lodge. Apart from 25, 5th street, there are 19, 21 and as many yards as there are odd numbers up to 35. There is no point in describing them. They are all like 25, 5th street. This is where we live and have our being. In all the odd numbers.

Sitting in the lodge is a brown woman. She is very hard. Everything about her says 'hard'. She is fattish, seally fat and you can see that under her dress, she wears a long line bra and girdle. You know that if you touch her, the compressed fat-beneath-the-bone would fail to give. She is hard. She never leaves her seat but you can, every second, hear the 'clang clang' as her crotchet needle hits against her thumb-nails. Intricate patterns she must be crocheting because it never ends. Hard up-standing woman. The doctors says she doesn't pee . . . stones in her bladder.

Government houses are built as the name suggests by the government for the people . . . for us the indigent, who have been made so by fire, hurricane or some other catastrophe. The house is a gift but on our shoulders lie the cost of its maintenance. To keep the roofs from springing leaks, the toilets and sinks in working condition, we the occupiers pay 25 cents every time we leave the premises. This is our responsibility; this is our contribution to our welfare.

Truth to tell, we hardly leave for we have no skills to offer and no funds to pay our exit fee. Miss D in the porter's lodge does the collecting. She is supposed to be Mr D's assistant but no one has ever seen Mr D. We suspect that she is also Mr D. She is as old as the scheme and has never been known to let through 24 cents. Miss D is hard. Beg her a chance, a cent just dropped through your fingers into the drain and she says "Wait 'til the cleaner man comes to clean it out, then bring me the right amount. I can't do that kind of thing. You want me to get in trouble nuh. You want Mr D to come kill me." The D's, in any case Miss D, must know how hard it is for us to find 25 cents. We came into the scheme with nothing . . . destitute. She has been at the lodge half-sharing our existence for centuries now. There is no way she could not know that.

Yes, it is a hard life however you look at it but we, at least, are trying. Egbert keeps our hearts warm with the promise of the second coming. Errol always finds time to tell us what is in those big volumes he is always reading and we hear about the millenium dawn when we shall truly rule ourselves. Barry doesn't read; he thinks it is bull shit. Pardon me but Barry is like that. But he thinks. He thinks we'll get a cross between the two — a second coming but a theocracy and then we'll be angels, black angels. Beatrice is rough: but never you mind; her bark is worse than her bite. She can always find time and cloth to make a bandage or two and to put a patch here and there and she is good with a darning needle and don't our small clothes need it!

I do my small part. I take the minutes of the regular weekly meetings.

There are some of us who don't try at all. No need to hide it. We have unfortunately to make a distinction between them and us. Those people throw dice, slam dominoes and give-laugh-for-peasoup all day long. They have no culture, no sense of identity, no shame or respect for themselves. Those people would climb through the barbed-wire fence, mingle shamelessly with the people beyond, beg them rum and cigarettes and creep back into the compound. They have no culture at all. No interest in helping their leaders keep their heads up high. We get no co-operation from them. How will we ever lead them out in the right and proper way, through the front gate, past the turnstile, past Miss D, proud, skilled, cultured and tall? Bad as she be Miss D knows who is who though. She never questions us when we ask for extra toilet paper and she makes every effort, over and beyond her call of duty to give us the books and writing paper that we need. She knows leadership when she sees it.

Jane and Louisa Will Soon Come Home, 46–51.

Please note that the action in this first piece takes place in a kind of living arrangement called a 'yard'.

Some public policy action that would be affected by the hypothesized disconnect, my thinking through my fiction led me to see, was the therapeutic. Many of the kinds of people who live in 'yards' are those seen by the State's social workers who are charged to effect their therapy. I designed the sociological study of yards in the city of Kingston, published in 1975 while I was thinking through and writing *Jane and Louisa Will Soon Come Home*, to see whether the assumed disconnect did indeed exist and manifest itself in that aspect of the therapeutic called problem-solving, an area which, for the best results, requires cooperation based on mutual understandings between the therapist and the client.

The research question was: Are there, in this 'yard' culture, systems of problem-solving which are unknown to those of us who have been propelled into another class and are now the agents of the state's therapeutizing intentions? We noted after our exposure to yard life that our people there did have such systems. It seemed logical to argue that if the State's agents are unaware of systems which the client uses, they are quite likely to impose their definition of solutions on their clients, leaving these clients to operate a system which they do not understand, and forcing them to abandon what they do know and what could possibly be repaired, for what will now be dependency on other/State solutions, in the process disparaging the knowledges that they have.

My preliminary hypothesis was now extended to read:

...in the interest of economy, self confidence and eventual social unity, the State should know and valorize native solutions, improve them where necessary and insert them into the development process.

I took this as my own charge and went back into the field to produce 14 volumes of life histories of Jamaicans born at the turn of the twentieth century. Both the conceptualization of this work and its concretizing were fuelled by the understandings which came to me while writing *Jane and Louisa*, that to know ourselves and the path forward we have to listen to our ancestors. I shall read a small bit.

Having decided that there was no future in staying with the brothers in the yard, Nellie, the novel's major character, the minute taker, wanders until she meets the ancestors.

> There were scores behind them popping up, popping up like geometric progression or the Gordon's ad....'You see not one piper but one hundred'. And so it was. Everybody playing the same note:
> -What happen?-
> It was art, from any angle...music, shape, production, performance, colour scheme, blending of colours, a pageant. They broke into sections as often in choral speaking:
> - Have you seen Locksley, Letitia's boy?-
> -Have you seen Uroy, B's son by Stanley's boy?-
> -What is Uriah doing with himself?-
> -Did Teena really name the child Obadiah after me?-
> Names all familiar but I couldn't put faces to them. I wasn't in touch. I couldn't see well enough yet.
> -She isn't in touch. She isn't in touch. She can't see well enough yet-
> Like Gilbert and Sullivan, a conductor-less orchestra, as the contralto, soprano, bass ride the nonsensical chorus:
> -She isn't in touch. She isn't in touch. She can't see well enough yet- I wasn't in touch. I was looking at the splendour of it all.
> Then a tall one in the back spoke rather than sang:
> -I hear they no longer make banana mullum-
> Banana mullum. What's banana mullum, I was thinking when the whole chorus softly, then rising to a crescendo, sang:
> -What's banana mullum. She don't know banana mullum- They just about used my exact words. They weren't just putting on a performance for me. They were trying to communicate. They were picking their way through my brains. I listened.
>
> *Jane and Louisa Will Soon Come Home*, 79–80.

A thesis concerning development issues and Caribbean public policy finally emerged from the writing of fiction and active field work. It can be found in the recently published work *The Second Generation of Freemen in Jamaica 1907–1944*. A comment from an informant in St. James recorded in this book, 'de old people dem no like how oonoo dish out first of August', is one of the most poignant statements establishing the actual existence of the disconnect between those managing development and those to be managed, as modelled in the first reading. A review of the several Governors' actions, coupled with the analysis of the life histories of such as the informant quoted above, approached the concern about identifying the elements in the disconnect. The data found them to be lodged in the colonial approach to governance, and especially in the education system it encouraged. *Jane and Louisa's* fictional representation of the brothers in the yard and their elitist and socially divisive intellectual activity now moved from fiction to fact. From which direction of the social system would the change that had to be, come?

The meditation called *Myal*, which appeared in print in 1988, modelled this answer. Several years of hypothesizing and testing had brought me, among other things, to the understanding that a significant proportion of the people whom history and social and economic conditions cast in the role of petitioner for government aid, see themselves as African Jamaicans. Within the African-Jamaican world view, chronic problems are diagnosed as spirit-based: the enemy can steal your spirit and leave you not only ill but too dispirited to see that you are ill. The antidote is also spirit-based. The social problem of which disconnect is a part, from the native standpoint could be characterized as a spiritual struggle which the African Jamaicans had yet to win. I opined that the struggle would be won when the spiritual forces of all kinds came together as myalists, forces which had been working before as individuals. In *Myal* I therefore pull the Baptist preacher, Reverend Simpson (in his animal persona, called Dan), the herbalist, Mass Cyrus (in his animal persona called Percy), the four-eye man, Ole African (sometimes called Willie), the kumina queen, Miss Gatha (sometimes called Mother Hen) and two acolytes, Maydene (the foreign white woman recently discovered to be White Hen) and her half-caste Jamaican husband (the Methodist preacher who would be called Mongoose when he is admitted to the clan of Myalists) into one working group. Unlike the fellows in the yard in *Jane and Louisa*, the members of this spiritual group are all in their own ways in intimate contact with their people. I watch these characters as they define Jamaica's (the society's) problem, prescribe and operate. The subsequent charge is that one of them must infiltrate the high reaches of the society and, from that vantage point, subtly enter the education system and nullify its spirit-splitting potential.

A new hypothesis, Hypothesis 2, arose from this involvement with fiction:

> ...If the disconnect between developer and the developed is located in the colonial education and socializing system, and if it has to be treated by spiritual strength and if there are, within the culture, areas of spiritual strength, then those concerned with development issues and public policy in Jamaica and possibly the Caribbean should (a) define, locate and highlight these areas of strength; (b) produce new material based on the definition of this strength; and (c) pry from current educational material dispiriting elements and replace them with (b).

The first research tasks would be to locate these areas of strength. My action has not continued past this point .

Having realized from the work for the *Second Generation of Freemen* that the term African Jamaican was real, I concluded that much could be learnt about how to handle the social consequences of the history of the experience of kidnap, transportation, the auction block, slavery and a beggarly emancipation, and on the more concrete level, if units of people prefixed as African were to cooperate in producing a worthwhile black space. That sociological work, too, is still on the drawing board but the conceptualizing process which normally precedes the sociological has been published in the form of the novel *Louisiana*. The hypothesis grounding that work reads:

> ...If a large body of people have the same history they are likely to have similar problems adjusting to the societies in which they seek to be included, especially if those societies are similar. They could learn from each other's problem-solving efforts. To do this sensibly would require that public policy admit, into its thinking and action, the notion of an African diaspora and a shared culture of problem-solving.

Louisiana aimed, as a result, to imagine diasporan similarities as well as cooperative cultural productions in the hope of highlighting items which socio-historical research would later examine. *Louisiana,* the model, pictured only one other Africa-prefixed geographic location, African America. A shared cultural item pinpointed from this involvement with fiction, was the structure and function of spirituality and another was music. I read a small bit related to music.

> I am not Madam Marie. I don't engage my clients in arguments about the origins of their relationships with the songs they sing. I am Louisiana. After ten or so years with this clientele I know the songs and where we each learnt them. No need for argument. The songs are equally ours now. We just sing. I made no statement on this. It is the shape of things. My clients, though they are as many natives as West Indians, don't argue among themselves about origins either. I first noticed this funny departure with 'Prim strim stramma diddle'. Sheer nonsense if you ask me, but a common chord. The West Indian who had introduced it, had prefaced: "I learnt this song from the blackest man I have ever seen. It was as if someone had painted him in tar. He was from Barbados. A Baptist parson. He had served in West Africa." A man from Virginia said that he had no doubt that he had seen the very blackest man. He too was a parson who had been to Africa and was originally from the islands. Could the song be:

> Coy me menero
> kill Tukero

Coy mi nearo
Coy me
Prim strim stamma diddle
Lara bone a ring
Ting a rignum
Bulli dina coy me.

It was. Total nonsense. But there it was. A common chord. We hushed up after that.

Louisiana, 129–30.

The work in historical sociology linking African America and African Jamaica which I still hope to do, will have to see spirituality and music, among other items, as a possible site of cooperative creation, note their incidence and function in the historical existence of African Jamaicans and African Americans and see what of problem-solving behaviour inheres in these items.

Into such paths of fiction — *Jane and Louisa*, *Myal* and *Louisiana* — has my interest in development issues and Caribbean public policy led me. Give thanks for the fiction. Where the model *Jane and Louisa* had its sociological companion in the *Second Generation of Freemen in Jamaica 1907–1944*, *Myal* has not had its own. *Myal* should have been followed by an in-depth study of school, college and university curricula, their teaching material, methodologies and messages to descendants of Africans enslaved in the New World, and by a review of the culture, which review would indicate its spiritual strength. This has not been done, and *Louisiana* has yet to have its published work on African American–African Jamaican relations. Sociological works which address development issues and public policy need cartloads of data, and this in turn requires institutional support. After 1985 and my exit from the University of the West Indies and institutional support, this was difficult for me. The models, *Myal* and *Louisiana*, have had to stand alone.

Several sculptors have drawn images which did not get to the wood, stone or steel, and the messages they hoped to broadcast have had to be abandoned in a drawer. Several dress designers' sketches have not seen the catwalk, and the beauty they hoped to share has been left in a filing cabinet. My models have, fortunately for my message, been accepted as literary art, given an audience and a life of their own, due largely to my sister Velma Pollard's insistence that *Jane and Louisa* was literary art.

With the knowledge that the models have a validity of their own, with self-funding evaporating and with other sources difficult to see, will my fiction still be hypotheses/models? I think not. I am getting the signal that I have reached the end of this style. Now I try to write material that is more accessible to the people with whom I live. In this and other ways I try to learn from my past fiction and make myself a Myalist rather than an appendage to the brother-in-the-yard.

Cyar Take Dat

BROTHER RESISTANCE

I wuk me finga to de bone fo mi country
I squeeze blood out a stone fo mi country
De people in authority
Mashing up me family
So much of de earth
Have we sweat and toil
Is we blood and tears wey till de soil
But we still suffering today
And we children cyar see deh way

A wake up in de morning an is unemployment
A cyar take dat
A wake up in the morning an is more retrenchment
A cyar take dat
When dey go to stop all dis humiliation
A cyar take dat
A wake up in the morning an is more frustration
A cyar take dat

No!
Ain't taking dat so
De people ain't takin dat, uh

Ain't taking dat so
De people ain't takin dat, eh, eh…

A love to live but meh life is a scramble
I have nothing to put a bread on meh table
You mock democracy
Licking up meh dignity
So much o hungry mout to feed
Is we cry blood just to sow de seed
But we still suffering in pain
An we children feeling de strain

Eh!?
A wake up in de morning an is unemployment
(signals audience to respond) A cyar take dat,
Mmm
A wake up in the morning an is more retrenchment
(audience) A cyar take dat
Lord, when dey going stop all dis humiliation
(audience) A cyar take dat
Eh? A wake up in the morning an is more frustration
(audience) A cyar take dat

No!
Ain't taking dat so
De people ain't takin dat, lawd
Ain't taking dat so
De people ain't takin dat, eh, eh…

A ha to cut it from the belly of de nation
You mash me corn an it cause aggravation
Life worth o poverty
Is endless agony

A lot oil dat we sacrifice
Don't get togedda and we pay de price
But we mus get justice today
So we children could see dey way

A wake up in de morning an is unemployment
A cyar take dat
A wake up in the morning an is more retrenchment
A cyar take dat
When dey going to stop all dis humiliation
A cyar take dat
A wake up in the morning an is more frustration
A cyar take dat

No!
Ain't taking dat so
De people ain't takin dat, uh
Ain't taking dat so
De people ain't takin dat, eh, eh…

So give us this day our daily bread
Because a hungry man…?
(audience) Is a angry man.
(Resistance) A hungry man?
(audience) Is a angry man.
(Resistance) An de people ain't taking dat at all, at all, at all…hmm!

A Big Dutty Lie

A big dutty lie, a big dutty lie
A big dutty lie, tell Columbus goodbye
A big dutty lie, a big dutty lie
We done had enough of the big mamaguy

So tell me weh di cause for de celebration?
When all deh bring de Caribs dem was aggravation
Their lust and deh greed and deh destruction
De stress and disease to de population
Damn liar! You tell one lie and it lead to another
Tief people land den say deh discover
Come down on a mission was to rape and plunder
Satisfy you hunger for gold and silver … eh, eh, eh

A big dutty lie, a big dutty lie
A big dutty lie, tell Columbus goodbye
A big dutty lie, a big dutty lie
We done had enough of the big mamaguy

So tell me weh di cause for de celebration?
When all dey bring de Caribs dem was aggravation
Their lust and dey greed and dey destruction
De stress and disease to de population
Damn liar! Dey want we to forget bout de days of slavery
I have a duty to tell de true story
Five hundred years of colonial agony
Dey not goin to crown no pirate to glory

A big dutty lie, a big dutty lie
A big dutty lie, tell Columbus goodbye

A big dutty lie, a big dutty lie
We done had enough of the big mamaguy

So tell me weh di cause for de celebration?
When all deh bring de Caribs dem was aggravation
Their lust and deh greed, their lust and deh greed and deh destruction
De stress and disease to de population
Damn liar. De Pinta, de Niña, de Santa Maria
Take up Europe wid a cargo a gangsta
Come down on a mission was to rape and plunder
Anywhere deh land up de say *(spoken)* "We discover"

(spoken)
Is a lie so big
Is a lie so big even History believe it
Even History believe it

Why?

(singing Chaka Demus & Pliers tune)
History book take bad character
Change up the look for we to admire
History book take bad character
Change up the look for we to admire
He look pretty, he look so pretty but he character ... *(pause for audience to respond)*
Look so pretty, he look so pretty but he character ... *(audience)* dirty
Look so pretty, he look so pretty but he character ... *(audience stronger)* dirty!

Murder he wrote, murder he wrote
Murder he wrote, murder Columbus wrote

So goodbye Columbus
Leh we kiss him *(kisses air to the right)*
Goodbye Columbus
Leh we kiss him *(kisses air to the left)*

(spoken)
Yu tink we done?
Yu tink we done?
(chanting)
Goodbye Columbus LET WE KICK HIM!

(spoken)
Shall I kick him again? *(audience)* Yes!
Kick him again? *(audience)* Yes!
(It have violence in dis room bwoy!)
Kick him again?! *(audience)* YES!!
(chant) Goodbye Columbus, leh we KICK HIM!

A big dutty lie, a big dutty lie
A big dutty lie, tell Columbus goodbye
A big dutty lie, a big dutty lie
We done had enough o yu
We done had enough o yu
(spoken) We done had enough o yu big mamguy

Leh we get rid of Columbus and get on with de rest o we life
Give thanks.

Encounters with Poetry

Cecil Gray

I

The writing life, it seems to me, comes from the reading life.

One of the many lucky things that recurred in my life was that I kept brushing up against poetry. In primary schools in Trinidad then, you had to practise reading aloud from the Nelson's *West Indian Readers* by J.O. Cutteridge, the Director of Education there. Each week had its own 'lesson' and several of the 'lessons' were poems, beginning with things like 'A Naughty Boy' by John Keats at age 7:

There was a naughty boy
And a naughty boy was he
He ran away to Scotland
The people for to see –
There he found
That the ground
Was as hard
That a yard
Was as long,
That a song
Was as merry...
As in England.

We were never told to memorize the lines, nor recite them. But the delight we found in rhyme and rhythm had me and my classmates going around chanting them. And we got the message too, that what we had was as good as others. (One remembers Sparrow's calypso ridiculing the Cutteridge books, but one suspects Sparrow never went beyond 'Dan is the man in the van'. Perhaps he did not see the seed of self-respect planted there.)

Between the ages of 7 and 11 we were put in contact with poems and excerpts by Tennyson, Browning, Masefield, Wordsworth, Longfellow and Tom Redcam of Jamaica.

As 10-year-old boys we were told Tom Redcam of Jamaica was a disciple of Wordsworth — which of course meant nothing to us — but we still enjoyed his poem 'The Mothers of the City', the first four lines of which, at least, many of us stored in memory:

> _What is the noise that shuffles_
> _On the roads that lead to the town,_
> _While the city slumbers deeply,_
> _While the hours lie dumbly down . . ._

By age 11, incredible as it seems today, we were reading excerpts from Shakespeare's _King John_ and _The Merchant of Venice_ with a sufficient degree of understanding. We went around repeating 'The quality of mercy is not strained – / It droppeth as the gentle rain from heaven.' But more exciting to us were 'The Sea King's Burial' by Charles McKay and 'Alexander Selkirk' by William Cowper.

If you go to Trinidad for Carnival you might see a masquerader disguised as a Robber who might stop you with these lines from 'Alexander Selkirk':

> _I am monarch of all I survey,_
> _My right there is none to dispute._
> _From the centre all round to the sea_
> _I am lord of the fowl and the brute._

As well-remembered, in a different way, were two others. One was Longfellow's 'The Day Is Done' which begins:

The day is done, and the darkness
Falls from the wings of Night,
As a feather is wafted downward
From an eagle in its flight.

The other was 'The Burial of Sir John Moore' by Charles Wolfe. For some reason the solemn funeral steps of that poem had us voluntarily reciting as much of it as we could, like little actors:

Not a drum was heard, not a funeral note,
As his corse to the ramparts we hurried.
Not a soldier discharged his farewell shot
O'er the grave where our hero we buried.

Not long ago a friend and I found ourselves saying that poem again, read 72 years ago in our primary school.

We never let grammatical inversions, archaic vocabulary or allusions bother us. We were finding delight in the sounds and movements of words. A delight that for me increased as the years went by.

At age 11 I had finished primary school with nowhere to go. The government offered free secondary schooling to four pupils who topped what was called the Exhibition Exam, precursor to the Common Entrance. Hundreds of primary pupils wrote that exam, all coached in private lessons for three or four years. My mother could hardly afford to buy me schoolbooks, far less pay for private lessons! So, though I was always in the top three of my class, all secondary school doors were closed to me. Poetry had had its day.

But fortune came to the rescue. After hanging on in school two more years, at age 13, despite my desperate protests, I was made a monitor in what was called the Pupil Teacher system. In that system you had to pass seven annual examinations — the fourth one a practical test — to earn a Provisional Teacher's Certificate. As a monitor I was merely to assist a teacher with little tasks like correcting spelling tests, but I was soon put fully in charge of a class: First Standard. So at 14 I began my teaching career as a Pupil Teacher. (Incidentally, I managed to come first in five of those exams.)

I say all that because it is related to my further exposure to poetry. For three of those exams three books of poetry had to be studied. They were called *Pattern Poetry* I, II and III. From those three books other influences came like 'Lord Randal', 'The Wife of Usher's Well' and other ballads; and like 'The Highwayman' by Alfred Noyes, and Tennyson's 'In Memoriam' for his dead friend, Arthur Hallam, ('Break, break, break / On thy cold grey stones, O Sea!'). Of course, I revelled in the sway of Masefield's romantic poem 'Sea Fever' ('I must go down to the seas again, to the lonely sea and the sky'). But another poem by Masefield, 'Cargoes', intrigued me more. The first stanza moves with the slow even motion of pre-Christian galleys:

Quinquireme of Nineveh from distant Ophir
Rowing home to haven in sunny Palestine ...

The second stanza brings us the feel of the sailing ships of the fifteenth and sixteenth centuries. Then the third stanza enters the twentieth century with the jerky progress of tugboats:

Dirty British coaster with a salt-caked smoke-stack
Butting through the Channel in the mad March days ...

That poem was, to me, a good example of how a poet could fit sound and rhythm to the sense. From that book too 'Dover Beach' by Matthew Arnold left its mark, though I did not understand the second part of it.

I think all that explains why, at about age 15, when I was receiving a stipend of six dollars a month, I bought a copy of Palgrave's *Treasury of English Verse* I saw in a bookshop and spent night after night with a kerosene lamp reading it.

It was the most eye-opening experience so far. I was thrilled, for example, by the sonorous grandeur of Coleridge's 'Kubla Khan' —

In Xanadu did Kubla Khan
A stately pleasure-dome decree:
Where Alph, the sacred river, ran
Through caverns measureless to man
Down to a sunless sea.

Then there was 'Elegy Written in a Country Churchyard' by Thomas Gray that lulled with its pentameters ('The Curfew tolls the knell of parting day, / The lowing herd wind slowly o'er the lea ...'), and had these lines everyone knows — 'Full many a flower is born to blush unseen, / And waste its sweetness on the desert air.' And a poem by W.B. Yeats that I memorized and carried with me for many years: 'When you are old and grey and full of sleep, / And nodding by the fire, take down this book, / And slowly read, and dream of the soft look / Your eyes had once, and of their shadows deep'.

Let me stress, in those adolescent years it did not seem a hindrance if everything was not crystal clear in every poem. I had not yet met people who thought you had to be able to explain every allusion in a poem to react to what it was conveying. I am reminded here of a teacher who told me once she could not present a certain poem to a class of 14-year-olds because she did not have the notes her university lecturer gave her. It was one of the many, many occasions I felt a surge of gratitude for not having gone to a secondary school. The library was my teacher.

Between the ages of 12 and 16, I spent a lot of time in the public library and read, among other things, the twenty volumes of the *Children's Encyclopaedia*, in each of which there were many poems. One that affected me a lot was 'The Bull' by Ralph Hodgson. It's a long poem that tells how a young bull dispossessed the old leader of the herd. Perhaps it was too sentimental an influence but I confess it was very moving at the time:

> *See an old unhappy bull,*
> *Sick in mind and body both,*
> *Slouching in the undergrowth*
> *Of the forest beautiful,*
> *Banished from the herd he led,*
> *Bulls and cows a thousand head.*

And so on for 180 lines.

In those years in all our islands and in British Guiana there was a great interest in things literary, even though a lot of it was hypocritical posturing, pretensions to Culture with the capital C. Still, the debating and literary clubs and groups compelled activities such as short-story writing, verse writing, debating and recitation. In Trinidad there was a League of Literary Clubs. Such clubs died a natural death as a more critical and knowledgeable outlook grew in certain quarters. They evolved into two or three groups of people who had a true interest in and an informed familiarity with literature.

When I was in my twenties in Port of Spain I became active in The Readers' and Writers' Guild. I am not clear when the Guild started. When I was involved in it, it was a forum where emerging writers like George Lamming, Sam Selvon, Cecil Herbert, Eric Roach, Douglas Archibald, Ernest Carr, A.M. Clarke, Harold Telemaque, John Wickham and others met, read some of their work, and talked.

Every six months or so the latest issue of *Bim*, the Barbadian literary magazine, was discussed. I was listening now to voices that spoke of things West Indian. It was there that a poem, 'In Our Land', by Harold Telemaque of Tobago awoke a fire in me —

> *In our land,*
> *Poppies do not spring*
> *From atoms of young blood,*
> *So gaudily where men have died;*
> *In our land*
> *Stiletto cane blades*
> *Sink into our hearts,*
> *And drink our blood.*

In the late 1940s and early 1950s the poetry of Derek Walcott and many other emerging poets got enthusiastic attention. We began speaking of West Indian Literature.

And that brings me to Frank Collymore of Barbados. His name stands high in the story of our literature. He was a poet, an actor, a short-story writer, a bit of a lexicographer, but above all the great gatherer of talent, great and small, wherever it sprouted at that time. He was a teacher at Combermere School out of which, beginning in 1942, he and Therold Barnes put out the magazine they called *Bim* (short for Bimshire, a nickname used for Barbados). Being a white Barbadian, he was able to get merchants, manufacturers and plantation owners to fund its publication by paying for advertisements in a few of its pages.

But if *Bim* started as a Barbadian magazine it was not that for long. Colly saw to that. It was in those pages the names of Derek Walcott, George Lamming and Kamau Brathwaite first drew attention. Later on, Mervyn Morris, John Figueroa, Edward Baugh and others appeared. Collymore trawled the entire Caribbean for writers. He almost always published what was sent to him, and was probably the first person to proclaim Derek Walcott a world poet at age 19. I am looking forward to the biography of Colly that Prof Baugh is now working on.

We cannot place too much importance on *Bim* — and on *Focus*, *Kyk-over-al*, and *Savacou*, all collectors of West Indian literary fruit — not only to remember the past but to consider the future.

With *Kyk-over-al* in Guyana A.J. Seymour was endeavouring to do what Collymore was engaged in. When Seymour fell ill *Kyk* languished. It came back to life later under the editorship of Ian MacDonald, until other difficulties arose.

Focus, the magazine edited by Edna Manley, excited me when I first saw the 1956 issue in 1959. It was doing for Jamaica what *Bim* had been doing since the 1940s, and from its pages I absorbed poems by M.G. Smith, George Campbell, H.D. Carberry, Ken Ingram, Basil McFarlane, Evan Jones, Vivian Virtue, Barbara Ferland and so on. I was particularly drawn to Barbara Ferland's 'Le Petit Paysan' and 'Expect No Turbulence', but I raved about 'Nature' by H.D. Carberry (perhaps 'raved' is too heavy):

We have neither Summer nor Winter
Neither Autumn nor Spring.
We have instead the days
When the gold sun shines on the lush green canefields —
Magnificently.

A different sentiment from Telemaque's 'In Our Land' but just as much our own.

About the time I discovered *Focus* I also came upon a little book, *A Treasury of Jamaican Poetry*, edited by J.E. Clare McFarlane. It was published in 1949 when he was president of The Poetry League of Jamaica. I found it a treasure indeed. Many of the poets I have already mentioned were there, as well as Agnes Maxwell Hall, Una Marson, Constance Hollar, Reginald Murray, and, above all, Claude McKay and his poems of nostalgia. I soaked myself in ones like 'I Shall Return' and of course 'Flame-Heart': 'So much have I forgotten in ten years, / So much in ten brief years! I have forgot / What time the purple apples come to juice, / And what month brings the shy forget-me-not'.

I cannot tell you how McKay's poems affected me then, especially when a few years later I obtained a copy of his *Selected Poems* and read ones like 'Home Thoughts', 'My Mother', 'The Harlem Dancer' and 'If We Must Die'.

> *If we must die, let it not be like hogs*
> *Hunted and penned in an inglorious spot,*
> *While round us bark the mad and hungry dogs*
> *Making their mock at our accursed lot. . . .*

No wonder Winston Churchill quoted it!

Of course I continued to read avidly poets such as Hardy, Day-Lewis, MacNeice, Spender, Frost, and so on. I found 'Musée des Beaux Arts' by W.H. Auden unforgettable:

> *About suffering they were never wrong,*
> *The Old Masters: how well they understood*
> *Its human position; how it takes place*
> *While someone else is eating, or opening a window or just walking*
> *   dully along ...*

The less traditional poets fascinated me. D.H. Lawrence, for example, in 'Snake':

> *A snake came to my water trough*
> *On a hot, hot day, and I in pyjamas for the heat,*
> *To drink there.*

In the deep, strange-scented shade of the great carob-tree
I came down the steps with my pitcher
And must wait, must stand and wait, for there he was at the trough
  before me.

At the end of the 1960s Kamau Brathwaite gave us his trilogy: *Rights of Passage*, *Masks* and *Islands*. I still have a vivid memory of being at the Little Theatre on Tom Redcam Avenue and hearing Kamau read 'Negus' from *Islands*. Walcott gave us *The Gulf* about that time, and some years later *The Fortunate Traveller*. His 'Season of Phantasmal Peace' became a great inspiration.

II

In 1959, not long after the University of London gave me a degree, I was sent here to Jamaica to do the Diploma in Education. As part of the exam I had to write two Advanced Essays (as they were called). I wrote one on the teaching of West Indian history and the other on the teaching of West Indian poetry. It seemed to me it was criminal then not to teach West Indian Literature in West Indian schools.

So in 1960 when luck made me a lecturer I made it my mission to introduce teachers to West Indian poems that seemed eminently suitable to present to their students. I put together a little booklet of cyclostyled poems that included Dennis Scott's 'Uncle Time' and 'Bird', Anthony McNeill's 'Ode to Brother Joe', Mervyn Morris's 'The Pond' and 'The Roaches', H.D. Carberry's 'Nature', Ian McDonald's 'Jaffo the Calypsonian', A.L. Hendriks's 'Road to Lacovia', Lamming's 'Birthday Poem For Clifford Sealy', Derek Walcott's 'A Letter from Brooklyn' and 'A City's Death By Fire' and others. And we discussed possible ways of dealing with them in class. Of course, on my visits to their schools I tried to make the best suggestions I could in the actual classrooms.

Word got around that I was spouting some new ideas, and I was approached by publishers about putting out books. I compiled a book of West Indian stories I called *Response*, chosen to get an involved response from young West Indian students to things in their own lives they could identify with. It was published in 1969. Just about then, Ken Ramchand asked me to join him in doing the anthology called _West Indian Poetry,_ which came out in 1971. Then came the three books of poems that I called _Bite In,_ which some teachers are still using in many of the islands. This was all part of the reading life, since I searched sources wherever English was written. Several of the poems, however, came from the magazines _Bim, Focus,_ and _Kyk-over-al._

But there was a war to be fought. There were the defenders of colonial bastions to deal with. 'What about standards?' they asked, as if being West Indian naturally meant mediocrity. It was the teachers who won that war.

When I was asked to be chairman of the panel to prepare the CXC English syllabus there was little opposition to the idea of including West Indian poems and stories. Before and after that, each of the many textbooks I put out was at least seventy per cent West Indian.

I am reminded now that someone in the 1950s said that a study of the West Indies is a study of poverty. Perhaps that's not so true today, but I seem to see the ravages of a literary poverty spreading. Why is most of our writing being done abroad?

West Indian literature blossomed when Frank Collymore, A.J. Seymour and Edna Manley saw the necessity for the magazines they put out. I think we ought to learn something from that. I think UWI has a responsibility in that regard. There is a crying need for _Bim, Focus,_ and _Kyk-over-al_ today. Whatever is here now in the soil has to be watered by recognition and encouragement. Isn't it time UWI put out an annual magazine of creative writing, as the University of The Virgin Islands does? Not a journal of reviews; we already have that. But one with the new voices asking if anyone is listening. Where are the successors to John Hearne, Martin Carter, Lorna Goodison, Olive Senior, Mervyn Morris to be welcomed and noticed?

I can hear the question, 'Where are the readers to support such a magazine?' And that brings us to what I consider the key to the future of poetry in our territories. It is readers who must keep that poetry alive and it is readers who become the poets. So where are the readers to come from? I believe they come out of what happens in the secondary schools. The classrooms where teachers present poems in a way that lets the poems arouse real emotional responses are the classrooms likely to send out people who go to poetry for a pleasure not found elsewhere. They are the people likely to become lifelong readers. If we are at all interested in the continuing flowering of West Indian poetry we must look critically now at what is being done in our secondary schools.

Writing Against the Grain

KENDEL HIPPOLYTE

To say that I am a writer says little more than to indicate that in some way part of my life's normal activity involves getting words onto paper for reasons which are not strictly functionally related to a salary or wage paid by some external organization. Even that cautious semi-negative definition must give me pause now. I've just gone into a radio drama project with scriptwriting as one of my duties, and as scriptwriter I will be paid per script. All right, not a fixed salary or wage, but it raises the apparently-obvious-and-yet-not-really question of how that kind of writing may still entitle me to call myself a writer — whereas someone who, say, writes project proposals as a substantive part of his or her daily activity will not be thought of as a writer. And it seems to me that the question — what is a writer? — is resolved precisely in this notion/image of writing against the grain.

Against the grain of what? And if there is writing against the grain, is there, by logical inference, writing with the grain? Who does that? What distinguishes the two kinds of writing? I hope there are clear answers to these innocuous questions, but I doubt it. But let us assume they must be explored — although whether they *must* be explored is perhaps the most important question that should be explored. However …

If I go back to my writer of project proposals, he, if reasonably articulate, could both explain and justify his work to customers in a bar or shoppers at a supermarket. People might quarrel over the value, that is social utility, of a particular project, but the basic activity of conceiving and writing project proposals is socially useful in a way that barflies and shoppers can accept and they will not quarrel unduly over whether the person should receive a salary. Whereas I would have a very hard time explaining and justifying why I should be paid a salary for staying home and writing poems. Quite frankly, I would have a hard time explaining and justifying it to myself, so I sympathize deeply with the barflies and shoppers. But this notion of the social utility of writing, and therefore of the writer, is what I want to take as my touchstone in exploring this idea of writing against the grain. And the figures of the project proposal writer and the poet are handy to keep in mind as contrasting images on either side of the issue of social utility.

Seamus Heaney has a wonderful poem, 'Digging', which among other things affirms a faith in the social value of writing. Thinking of his father, and grandfather before him, handling their spades masterfully in the unquestionably necessary work of growing food, at the end of the poem he says:

> *But I've no spade to follow men like them.*
>
> *Between my finger and thumb*
> *The squat pen rests.*
> *I'll dig with it.*

Quarrel with it if you like, but there, unmistakably, you have it: a faith in the social utility of the writer — and not just the writer, but that apparently most parasitic and self-indulgent of the species, the poet. How does one, living and writing in the Caribbean, arrive at such a faith? And if you do arrive at it, how do you sustain it?

Understand me clearly here. I am talking about social utility. I am not talking about the value of writing *for the writer.* On that, I am quite clear. Even just at the practical level, I know why writing is necessary for me. I'm too muddle-headed and woolly a thinker to trust myself to somehow keep track of my inner life. And I've learned that when I lose track of my inner life, I start to lose interest in the outer one. So I find that, to keep my practical outer life going, I need to write, since it keeps me in touch with the inner reasons for keeping that outer life going in the first place. Admittedly, it goes deeper than that to the nature of that inner life and why I believe it's important to keep track of it. But I will come back to that later. I think, though, that any writer, in the sense in which I am using the word, understands the personal value, indeed necessity, of writing for a coherent inner life. But for now we are considering the writer as a social figure, not a private individual, and therefore must face the troublesome (and from a certain viewpoint, even crass) issue of social utility.

Here, situating oneself as a figure in the social framework, the image of writing against the grain takes on a particular cogency. Seamus Heaney's faith is genuine and inspiring, but can we really believe that in the Caribbean the activity of a poet matters to the society? I focus on the poet as the archetype of the writer precisely because the degree of isolation, separateness from social process that _may_ constitute a poet's journey (and I stress 'may') is simply not likely for a novelist and even less likely for a playwright. So, does the poet's work have social utility? Does that depend on the poet and the type of poetry? Rather than generalize prematurely, I'll begin to explore the answers along a more autobiographical route: Do _I_ believe that my activities as a poet in Saint Lucia have social utility, social value? I do. But why do I believe that? A self-protective, merciful egotism? Some of that probably is there, but it seems to me I have reason to think there's more to it than that. And a full answer requires me to give a fairly concrete idea of what these 'activities as a poet' actually are.

What are my activities as a poet in Saint Lucia?

Well, for one thing, I take part in literary readings/performances of various kinds. Over the years, there have been phases where these are pretty regular, say once every two months, occasionally more often. Sometimes I'm just a participant, sometimes I'm involved in the organizing. These readings/performances vary in provenance: they may be the end of month readings at the Castries Central Library of a great and struggling little group called the Writers Forum; or for a while, close to a year, there was a bar in

Castries called The Garage in a semi-sleazy, evocative backstreet that did a weekly Culture Night (on a Thursday, I think it was) and all kinds of dubious types would wander in to perform original poems, songs, sometimes accompanied by drum and/or guitar; an adventurous dancer might do a solo; I remember one time a jazz trumpeter — from Norway, if I remember rightly — walked in out of the blue and just blew his mind and ours for a while; but poetry was always the anchor, and I was a regular performer there while it lasted. A couple of other places tried to imitate The Garage, but they lacked the spirit and never caught on. So that was one kind of forum. Another kind, totally different, is the grand national occasion — Emancipation, Nobel Laureate Week, that kind of thing, and I usually perform at those too.

So that's part of my activity as a writer — the more public aspect, if you like. And I think it's socially useful because it helps to normalize the idea of the writer as a natural, inevitable part of a society. Out of that kind of public activity, people — grandfathers and little girls in school uniforms — will meet you on the street and say: 'I saw you doing the poem on the Square, Emancipation Day.' The public aspect helps to cultivate a tradition. And a literary tradition, oral and scribal, because it encodes aspects of the inner life of an entire people, is a tremendous gift for a country to have available for its citizens. I think now of Martin Carter, who has a beautifully bittersweet piece called 'The Poems Man':

> *Look, look, she cried, the poems man,*
> *running across the frail bridge*
> *of her innocence.*

It came apparently out of an actual incident in which a little girl running by did in fact call out that phrase when she saw him. I like to know that kind of thing is possible and to help make it more possible.

There are other activities, less public, but still associated with the public aspect: judging a school's elocution competition in which at least some local work is used; performing at schools during Reading Week. All very necessary for nurturing a tradition.

Another part of my activities can be loosely labelled as 'mentoring'. That same Writers Forum referred to earlier meets on Tuesdays 7:30 p.m. at the Central Library, and I have an ongoing connection with them. I've done structured workshops, organized workshops using other tutors; sometimes I just go and sit in on the sessions and I may participate fully or just observe with an occasional comment. Or a school may have a literary club and I'll be invited to come and do a session of some kind. At the community college where I teach, my wife and I have designed and taught courses in poetry and we've brought out two anthologies of students' work. There was for a couple of years a vibrant writers group at the college. And so on.

And of course people, individuals of varying individuality — and talent — are always trying to get you to look at their poems or short stories or whatever. Increasingly my response has been 'Come to the Writers Forum sessions, we'll deal with it there', but sometimes I deal with it more personally than that.

So the activities I've mentioned give me reason to believe that as a writer I have some social utility. And while I've focused on autobiography here, the picture I've painted is relevant in varying degrees to other writers, like McDonald Dixon, John Robert Lee, Jane King, Travis Weekes, Ras Isley...

So if I'm socially useful, why this constant sense of 'against the grain'? What precisely is the problem?

For one thing, a deep-settled and unsettling awareness that you're not giving it your best. In fact you're not giving anything your best. You know that. You know that partly at least by some of the poems that you dream of — which can induce in you a despair at ever being able to bring together all the elements, internal and external, needed to write them. The external elements? The usual: time, solitude.

In spite of love
desire to be alone
haunts him like prophecy.

The opening lines from an early Mervyn Morris poem, 'Family Pictures', lines which lodged in my head the very first time I ever read them; they ring all too true, they twist the double-edged knife of artistic commitment and domestic guilt. Writing against the grain means (to change the image rather abruptly) being on the pendulum that swings you toward the poem and then, after an intense suspended pause (trying to put as much down as possible), carries you back toward home. This image of the pendulum makes it seem as though it is only the most minute fraction of time that one is fully a poet or fully a husband, lover, father. The rest of the time you're at varying distances from the ideal of either. And truly, that is often how it feels. Even though you know that from a certain vantage point, hard to reach, all this is a complementarity of experiences, more often than not it feels like a clashing of opposite forces in which you shuttle back and forth as a negotiator.

This can be a core experience for the writer, even for those who are able to give it almost full-time attention, far less the majority who must pay homage to Caesar between 8:00 a.m. and 4:00 p.m. or whatever one's working hours are. That's another opposing force to be negotiated with. And there are others, naturally — other relationships, other civic roles which at times must become the enemy. The simple truth is, as we all know, that no matter how much public good writing may do, how much social utility it may have, the process itself is irremediably antisocial. And since societies keep themselves functioning largely through more or less organized group processes, the process of writing a poem must necessarily feel like going against the grain. So you move back and forth constantly between the act of writing and any one of its temporary polar opposites: family, job, friendship, neighbourliness, civic duty and so on. In time, of course, you school yourself to accept the inevitability of this, but it doesn't dispel the gnawing sense that nothing is getting your absolute best for long enough. For some seven years now, my inadequate solution has been to go to bed between 8:30 and 9:30 and wake up anywhere around 3:00 a.m., sometimes before, sometimes after, depending on how much sleep my body claims. It's inadequate because there are situations in which it simply is not feasible, like when you're rehearsing a play or you're invited out and it's not politic to say no. But it's been a helpful strategy. Here again, though, note the leitmotif; you're moving against the normal social rhythm. Writing against the grain.

A question I've asked myself is: Does _knowing_ that you aren't giving to writing the absolute best of your time and psychic energy further vitiate even what you could give in the circumstances? Is that knowledge itself, unavoidable though it is, a crucial reason for this sense of writing against the grain? Beyond the practicalities of logistics and negotiating conflicting loyalties, at a deeper level writing against the grain involves negotiating with, in a sense dancing with, a subtle incipient despair which whispers: 'Look, you won't finally see that dream realized. So why set up yourself for disappointment?'

The despair is subtle because it blurs the fine meandering line between the public role of poet and the private being of being a poet. I've sketched a quick incomplete outline of what the public role of a poet could look like. And yes, connected with that role (although I've felt no need to say it) is writing poems of quality which can connect with the public along shared lines of enquiry, concern, affirmation. That is part of the dream (Derek Walcott's line: 'I am your poet, yours'): to know that your poems actually — actually, not just in your desperate imagination — shape a people's sense of themselves, for instance the way that Martin Carter's have.

But that is part of the dream, not the whole, the lit side of the moon which we see, not the whole moon. The serpent of despair is subtle because it whispers of unrealizable dreams as though the meaning of being a poet is found wholly in the public role. It is not. Necessary as that is, with its complicated apparatus of publishing, reviews, readings, conferences and all that — the lit side of the moon — the private dimension is equally important. I suspect if a gun were put to my head to force me to choose, I would say it was finally more important. I don't believe, given the nature of existence, that the public and private can be separated, only differently emphasized. But what I wish to do now in fact is, having acknowledged the social utility of the poet (notwithstanding the difficulties of writing poetry) to insist on the value of poetry for the private being of the poet.

It is here, I think, that the poet and the project proposal writer have to finally part company. You see, difficult as the process of writing a poem may be, and granted that there are people one will never be able to convince of the social value of poets, it is possible, with a little tweaking, to make a case for the published poem and the project proposal as writing with the grain. In these days when the concept, if not the practice, of development is going through another paradigm shift away from basic Reaganomics, there's more room now than a couple decades ago to fit in the poet (and certain types of poet more than others) as part of a new development paradigm. The term 'cultural industry', for example, is a key which can open doors that used to be locked against poets not all that long ago. Poets can contribute, directly and indirectly, to the economy. We can become part of the tourism product, part of the unique cultural profile that each Caribbean country needs increasingly to help it compete in a rapidly globalized environment ... I'd better stop. This is beginning to sound like the opening rationale in a project proposal. The point, I assume, is clear. The public role of poetry is accruing social value, status and — strictly in that sense — can take its place, if not alongside, in the vicinity of, the project proposal as writing with the grain.

But what of the poem which is never published in any form? Which is seen by only a few of the poet's acquaintances? Or not seen at all? Of what value is that to the poet? One thinks here of the extreme example of Emily Dickinson — hundreds of poems, poetry of high carat diamond — almost completely unknown during her lifetime. Of what value were they to her, whispers the serpent.

And it is here that we encounter most truly the ultimate meaning of writing against the grain. Of what value were they to her? Of what value were Martin Carter's last poems to him?

As always, and not only at conferences like this one, we are engaged in the paradoxical exercise of speaking about and around something because there is no way to speak IT directly. Poets try to speak IT, knowing in a part of themselves that the attempt is doomed but inevitable and completely necessary. The attempt to speak IT is the way that the poet must walk to arrive at IT, even though there are no guarantees that you will. But there is no way to be a poet and not try. The IT, for the purposes and within the constraints of language, is perhaps better conceptualized as a harmony, an orchestration of the elements of your self, though the personal experiencing of it is a oneness, not a severalness. Writing against the grain, finally, is using words to 'collect my scattered skeleton', that surreal and yet eerily accurate image of Martin Carter's.

Why inner fragmentation is the norm, why the instinct for unity of being is yet so ineradicable, why it is so difficult, why it requires your whole life, why failure or — to be kind — partial success is the more likely outcome: the answers to these questions must necessarily be individually experienced, even when you pursue the answers ensconced within a conventional carriage of religion. What is true, however, is that for the poet the collecting of the scattered skeleton of self is done through poetry — or more precisely, poem by poem. In that individual, unnegotiably private dimension, each poem truly achieved, whatever its public import, is an act of personal psychic integration. The sense, almost physical, of things coming together, when a poem is in its process of completion, can be so profoundly satisfying as to sometimes arrive at the state that we call 'peace'. And when that happens, it is reason enough to be a poet — even if one never publishes a poem, does a reading or any of the things associated with the public role. But such faith, which you see so starkly in Tony McNeill's poetry, is quite rare. It goes against the grain and is maintained by writing against the grain.

I want to close with a poem which I probably should simply have read instead of taking up time with a paper. It's called *contra diction*.

Since we must hear and see the separate words before the truth they mean
can reach us, there is, always, a contradiction of each word
and the One Word, original, indivisible, which is unheard, unseen.

All words are a translation always from what is to what has been.
Even within the truest poem something was lost, a final meaning blurred,
since we must hear and see the separate words before the truth they mean.

A haze of language shimmering the mindscape hangs a diaphanous screen
so that we see all things through mist and every sound is furred
and the One Word, original, indivisible, is unheard, unseen.

A great poet once, knowing the preterlingual unity of things, tried thirteen
ways to, but could not, translate in poetry the complete perception of a blackbird
since we must hear and see the separate words before the truth they mean.

Yet is it language or the nature of the mind itself which comes between?
And if such division, separation is our essence, what in us is stirred
by the One Word, original, indivisible, which is unheard, unseen?

We are divided. Riven by time, by sense, our first cry is a keen
for a lost wholeness. Our language afterward is an attempt, magnificent, absurd,
to hear and see the separate words before the truth they mean,
to reach the One Word, original, indivisible, unheard, unseen.

Writing from the Caribbean

Kevin Baldeosingh

In 1996, my first novel was published by Heinemann in their Caribbean Writers Series. My second novel was published the following year, also by Heinemann. So I felt I was well on my way. I knew what my next five books would be about, and I was under the delusion that publication depended on things like vivid prose, truthful characterization, and good storytelling.

Now I know better. You have to understand, in order to be a successful writer anywhere you have to be either popular or in fashion. Much of what makes a book publishable and what drives sales has to do with fashion. Naipaul put in nicely when he described himself as the kind of writer people think other people are reading. Diana Athill, who was Naipaul's editor at André Deutsch for over twenty years, notes in her memoir *Stet*:

> For a time during the 50s and early 60s it was probably easier for a black writer to get his book accepted by a London publisher, and kindly reviewed thereafter, than it was for a young white person.

Now why was that? It was because in that period, with Third World countries becoming independent, there was high political interest, which led to literary interest, which in turn was based on the expectation that a whole new market for new fiction in India and Africa and the Caribbean would be opening up. Well, that didn't really happen, for a variety of reasons. One main one was the mishandling of the education system by

Third World governments; another was that all the eminent novelists were very literary, which helped stymie a culture of reading of indigenous writers. But, as far as the Caribbean goes, perhaps the main reason was that virtually all our novelists wrote from the metropole.

Now, remember, I'm talking about fifty to forty years ago. So what's the situation nearly half a century later? Why, most of our novelists live and write from the metropole. I am the only Trinidadian novelist under 45 who actually lives in Trinidad. And it's beginning to bother me. Because I'm starting to wonder if I am the only moron who wants to write books from here.

Now there are very good reasons why anyone who wants to be a Caribbean writer has to leave the Caribbean. You see, it's a principle of economics that returns to skills for the individual go up with the existing skill average in the society.

> If skilled workers can freely move wherever they want, then they will tend to congregate in places where they can match with lots of other skilled workers. The economy will exhibit strong concentrations of high skill in a few places, surrounded by large swathes of low skill.

Studies of US immigrant groups show that 'An individual belonging to an immigrant group that had a high average wage was more likely to have a high wage than an individual belonging to an immigrant group having a low average wage.' (This is not tautological, or else the individual's wage is determined solely by his skills.) 'The patterns found suggest that an individual's opportunity for matching other skilled individuals is as important as the individual's own skills' (William Easterly, *The Elusive Quest for Growth*). So an Indian surgeon will be paid more in the US where s/he can match with skilled nurses, anesthesiologists, medical technicians, even receptionists. The same is true of novelists, who can match with literary agents, publishers, booksellers, and other writers. You can't do that in the Caribbean.

But there's a price to pay on the part of the people that Caribbean —

and I will now add the adjective 'so-called' to that noun — so-called Caribbean novelists are writing about. You all know Naipaul's famous comment (from *The Middle Passage*):

> Living in a borrowed culture, the West Indian, more than most, needs writers to tell him who he is and where he stands. Here the West Indian writers have failed. Most have so far only reflected and flattered the prejudices of their race and colour groups. Many a writer has displayed a concern, visible perhaps only to the West Indian, to show how far his group is removed from blackness, how close to whiteness.... To the initiated, one whole side of West Indian writing has little to do with literature, and much to do with the race war. The insecure wish to be heroically portrayed. Irony and satire, which might help more, are not acceptable.... The Trinidadian expects his novels, like his advertisements, to have a detergent purpose.

I don't know that what Naipaul wrote of 44 years ago has changed much. And when you have a region's writers living elsewhere, you have a peculiar situation where those writers are writing *about* a people *for* other people. Like I said, fashion and politics dictate a lot of what gets published. The Caribbean isn't fashionable now, as it was back in the 1960s. Metropolitan publishers publish those writers who deal with the experience of the minority person in the metropole. Which is quite right, because publishers must publish for a readership. And even then the publisher has to have the writer recommended to her or know the writer personally. So we have a situation in which the readership of Caribbean authors isn't really Caribbean people, it's people in the metropole.

That's not the writers' fault and it's not the metropole's fault. It's our fault. Because, with advances in technology and globalization, there aren't any insurmountable reasons we can't have a regional publishing house for fiction. But we don't have one — Ian Randle notwithstanding — for another reason, which I'll illustrate with a quote from the excellent biography of Derek Walcott written by Bruce King:

> Although Walcott was a central figure in the generation that formed

West Indian literature — he was the one who stayed home, he was the one who created theatre groups, he wrote about the arts in the local newspapers, he was actively involved in the literary scene in Trinidad and St Lucia — his role was oddly neglected by the first intellectuals and critics who concentrated on novelists and those with clear social views.

King says 'Although'. But it's not 'although'. It's *because* Walcott was the one who stayed home and wrote in the newspapers that he was neglected. That's how I know I'm a moron. But there's an old rhyme about morons which I quite like. It goes: 'See the happy moron / He doesn't give a damn, / I wish I were a moron; / My God! Perhaps I am!' And me, I am quite happy, so far, to stay here and write.

Writing Home Away From Home

KWAME DAWES

Home is where I would want to die. Or at least where I would want to be laid to rest. This is an odd matter since I do have a faith that assures me that what happens to me after this passing will have nothing to do with the meeting of the spirits of the dead in my burial plot. Still, I understand that when I die I don't want to be first confronted with a Southern accent. I want people who see me as family, as one of them, to welcome me. I want to encounter the familiar. And today, the familiar is Jamaica. Yet home is where I plant my roots. I live in South Carolina and I do feel a strong connection to that place. My body of work would be quite different if I did not live in South Carolina. But South Carolina knows that I engage her as someone who has encountered her as an outsider working his way in. Even my South Carolina-based poems are imagined through the prism of Jamaica.

The poems in my collection *Wisteria* were a way into that society for me. I did not intend to write those poems when I first sat down to interview the women and men who came to be the subjects of the poems. I wanted to understand something about the community, about the society in which I was living, about its history and the way that things have changed or not changed over the years. But after each interview, I would go home and write poems to process what I had experienced in the interviews. Still, those poems were merely part of a large cluster of poems I was writing as

I started to experience the new culture and landscape and as I started to read about the history of the state, and especially as I started to make friends in the community. Writing in South Carolina has been part of my settling in South Carolina.

I suspect that had I settled in Miami or New York, I would have formed relationships with Jamaicans and other Caribbean people. Here in South Carolina, there is a forced immersion that takes place, an inevitable pressure to contend with the meaning of African Americanness where in other settings that would not have to happen. I am grateful for this. It has given me a great deal as a writer, and has helped me to discover the rich lines that cross geography and time with the African diasporic community.

So South Carolina is home, but not in the way that home becomes a place where one wants to die. It won't be that for me just yet. It could eventually become that. It may well become that if I ever leave the state. If I do leave I doubt very much that I will feel a twinge of nostalgia when I hear some 'beach music' on the radio, or when I smell the starchy sweetness of cooking grits or the heavy greenness of collards boiling in pork-laced juice, or when I experience the bleary-eyed congestion of an allergy attack during the pollen-yellow season. What I will miss is not what my children will miss. This has been their home for all their lives. I will miss friends, miss the familiarity of a certain kind of pace in daily life, the routines of my commute. Only in that way will I begin to understand the real 'homeness' of South Carolina for me.

Writers must always be both at home and away from home. That distance and closeness is what will create the tension and the space to make art. I write about Jamaica while being away, but I am also here. Exile is no longer the same. I am in Jamaica a lot. I read the papers weekly online, I am in touch with my family, I am invested in the culture, and I listen to the music. But even when I was in Jamaica, I wrote of Jamaica as someone looking in — someone discovering it so that I would not take anything for granted.

By now, my biography has gone ahead of me in the bifurcated way my origins are described: Born in Ghana, grew up in Jamaica, and so on. I have always lived as if I am from somewhere else or as if there is somewhere else to which I belong. In Ghana, my father's many stories about Jamaica, about growing up in rural Jamaica, playing cricket, milking cows, riding donkeys, and going to Jamaica College served as the narrative of another landscape that belonged to me. Perhaps it is because he always spoke of one day going home. We were all going to go home to Jamaica. It was not that my father longed to return to Jamaica. He spoke of that return as an inevitable occurrence, one dictated by the aging of his mother and by his desire that we should see Jamaica and see more of what he grew up with than we had in the short trip we had taken there when I was just an infant.

When we moved to England, Ghana became the effective home, and so I encountered England as a sojourner, as someone who was far from home. As young as I was, I think I was beginning to define the posture of difference, the posture of someone who could look at the world as both an outsider and as an insider. This 'gift' would find its greatest expression when we moved to Jamaica in 1971. This was a black country and it seemed, in many ways, quite familiar, and yet it was, in actuality, quite different. The language was completely different, the food was different and the spirit of the people was distinctly different. Jamaica's aggression, the quick trigger of anger, was matched only by the immediacy of friendships and connections. This was a society that wore its energies on the sleeve, and it was quite different from the mood in Ghana. I studied Jamaica as a survivor, as someone who needed to make friends, needed to understand the world I was now living in and as someone who had to find a way to make it feel like home. When asked, I would always say I was Ghanaian. Being an African in Jamaica in the 1970s was not always an attractive thing. And so the meaning of difference, the capacity for irony as a way to cope with the anger at the insults, was something I learned quite quickly.

This is why, when I began to write plays, I knew that I had to write them about Jamaica, but I also knew that I would have to learn the language and ethos of Jamaica in ways that would compensate for the fact that I had missed the first ten years of its independence — the first ten years, which, tellingly, represented the first ten years of my own life. Reggae music I knew as it began to gain ascendancy. I had missed the period when Rock Steady was king, and unlike many of my friends, I did not grow up in the Kingston where I could watch people dancing to ska music. What I learned of that music and that time came through the stories told to me by friends and through the very comprehensive record collection of a family friend who shared her music with us. I had to learn it all like an amnesiac trying to connect the missing links of his past. I used patois as I would use another language — with a care for syntax, with a constant suspicion that I did not always get it right. I would test it on others — on true Jamaicans just to make sure I had it right. I spoke patois routinely, and it helped that I was a boy and one who went to an all boys' school where that was the day-to-day language. Having learned patois fairly late in my life built in me a fascination with the way that language would change, and an even greater fascination with the source for many of the lexical items and the improvisational nature of coinages. I would keep careful track of words that seemed to have been invented by a boy in the school and that would have regular parlance for several years before falling away. Even as I was learning Jamaica as home, I was standing outside of this home and trying to understand it. I was settled, during this time, about Ghana as my home. And for that reason I did not have to do anything but indulge in some nostalgia and invoke its position as 'first home' when I needed to assert or justify my difference.

The benefits for a writer of learning to be outside while securing one's inside status are hard to deny. The pleasure of seeing things afresh and wanting to somehow preserve them, or at the very least repeat them, was a significant part of my drive to write. I always had something to write about. I looked at the world around me, listened to the conversations, paid keen attention to the names of trees and fruits and flowers, and found myself wanting to use them in the plays I was writing. To write about Jamaican life, I had to be inquisitive, I had to ask questions when I went to people's homes, I had to pay very careful attention to the history of the country and to the personal histories of people who lived in the country, and I gathered all of this information and fed it into my work. At first all of this was done clumsily and without adequate craft to manage it, but I knew I was onto something interesting and I knew that not many people were paying attention to the things I was discovering.

By the time I was in my twenties, I knew that only two places would be comfortably called home by me: Jamaica and Ghana. I call South Carolina home, but not in that long-term ancestral sense of the term. South Carolina is where I live, and when I travel, I do feel as if I am returning home when I hit the I20, look for my exit and then make my way into my neighbourhood. But Ghana and Jamaica are home in ways that South Carolina cannot be. The facts of my immediate ancestry, my roots, if you will, define those places as home. This would not change. When I left Jamaica, I was also leaving family there. When I considered 'going home' for vacations (rare as they were), Jamaica was the obvious destination. And when I began to write poems and stories, I could tell that they would begin in Jamaica. The very project of my art was to be a part of the West Indian writers club. I was going to write the new generation of West Indian literature and I was very comfortable with this task. Indeed, it was exactly the kind of project that I needed to fire me to work.

'Why do I write?' Often it is assumed that I write because my father was a writer. But if that was the single factor, all my siblings would have to be writers or frustrated non-writers. This is not the case. I do know that writing has always been an engaging habit of mine. Not writing poems. I hardly did that kind of thing until I was about sixteen years old. But I wrote letters — lots of letters to pen-pals around the world. And I played around with a coded journal for several years. I invented my own alphabet, a crowd of signs and symbols that I came to know by heart with practice. I was able to write long stretches of very secret and personal prose during my teen years in this script. I have no recollection of the key for this script now, and it would be exciting to find some of the old exercise books that contained my coded notes. But I write now because I read. I liked reading. I enjoyed the way that stories would transport me to other worlds and consume my imagination. I made a contract with books and reading, and it was a simple contract: Books are good, books are an unbelievable invention. Books are full of secret truths that are always available. Books will always be around me and I will always find new things in books. Books are good things. That embrace of the book, of literature, and by extension, of art, continues to make me want to write books. I did not know I would make books then, but I knew that making books was a good thing. Eventually, I would want to make books, and eventually I would make books.

This contract with books should not be taken for granted, because, I suspect, there are many people today (and there were many people then) who do not have such a positive relationship with books. Where I saw the source for the richest range of information about the world in books, they now see this in the internet. Where I did not have ready access to film or television, they have ready access to a rich array of films and television shows that can provide them with the emotional and intellectual richness that books gave me. I am not saying that these relatively new media did not exist for me (actually the internet did not), but I am saying that the level of availability of such material is strikingly different now than it was when I was growing up. And yet, I know that the experience of reading a novel or a collection of poems cannot be replicated by searching through You Tube or the 71 million blogs that exist on the internet today. There is still an intellectual and emotional quality to the good book, or, at the very least, its content, that is hard to deny.

Yet despite the fact that I liked books, I don't think I came to really appreciate books until I discovered West Indian literature. Fortunately, I did not discover West Indian literature as an academic phenomenon, but as works filled with stories that opened the world that I knew to me in beautiful ways. I have read *Miguel Street* so many times now that it is pointless counting, and every time I laugh with the same glee that I did when I first read it as a child. I found *Miguel Street, A Morning at the Office, In the Castle of My Skin, Voices Under the Window,* and *The Last*

Enchantment, on my father's shelves beside _The Poor Christ of Bomba_ and _Cry the Beloved Country,_ and so many other African novels. First I was fascinated by the fact that I knew some of the names of the authors because they were friends of my father. They really were not famous, so seeing them on the cover of books was always amusing and interesting to me. But I came to many of their novels not out of lofty literary interest, but out of a teenager's desire to find salacious literature in the pages of the hundreds of books on my father's shelves. As you can imagine, I hit pay dirt again and again. I was reading great West Indian literature without really understanding that I was doing so, and I was finding sex written about in explicit and immediately relevant ways all at the same time. Books were a good thing. Books were a very good thing. I found passages about cricket, about high school in Jamaica, about places in the island that I had visited; about political experiences that are still talked about today. In Andrew Salkey's novels written for young readers — particularly the set that I like to call the 'acts of God novels of calamity' — I enjoyed the journey into the recent past of Kingston, a past that I had been denied by the fact of my birth in Ghana. In Vic Reid's stories about Maroons and Maroon life in the hills of Jamaica, I read the fictionalized accounts of places that my primary school visited on excursions — Maroon Town where the abeng blower announced the gathering and where chickens were sacrificed and rum was sprayed into the air by wizened old men armed with machetes and ancient muskets, a place where our Pentecostal young grade-four teacher, Mrs Carrington, broke into tongues to protect us from the encroachment of evil. It was all in the books, the forests, the paths where the redcoats were spotted and picked off, the dense vegetation where the Maroons could hide and devise brilliant insurgent tactics. Books. Books were good.

There is much we can learn from our predecessors. They sought to establish themselves as writers in the world. (Most, like my father, were interested in reaching Jamaican, West Indian, postcolonial and/or Pan Africanist audiences, but appreciated also the value of acceptance in the British and/or American mainstream market.) They submitted work to international publishers, because there was very little publishing in the Caribbean. (This has not changed.) Out of their reality they created imaginative worlds. (They knew that art can transform reality, and make it seem 'more real'.) They saw themselves as part of a movement towards self-definition. They felt the need to counter existing narratives of the region.

These writers, in the spirit of independence, challenged the colonial hold on society and culture. There are other issues critical today. Jamaica is constantly changing. The cities are growing, the engagement with the world is becoming increasingly more complicated; the meanings of race, religion, gender, sexuality are shifting. Violence is at epidemic levels. Crime has grown far beyond the norms of the 1960s, 1970s and 1980s. The music is constantly changing, charting the shifts in society through metaphor, language innovation, and new rhythms. There is much that has happened and continues to happen in our society that can benefit from the poetic power of observation and contemplation that literature affords.

The Colour of Free

Staceyann Chin

The afternoon pins me vulgar on the canvas of my memory.

I am on my way home from class, when a circle of boys, quickly herd me through the open door of the boys' bathroom. One of them slams the door shut. Their intent is clear and I am far beyond frightened.

I try to calm my nerves by counting colours.

'You don't have no mouth fi talk now, eh? What happen? Pussy got your tongue?'

The question confuses me. How many of them are in here?   A dozen, maybe thirteen, I couldn't count with them right up against me.

Count! My brain is screaming. Count!

'Why you so frighten a de big bamboo? You think it goin hurt you? It not goin hurt you, you know, just make you get back to normal, quick!' White Shirt moves closer to me. The circle moves in.

Stay focused. Pay attention to the faces!

Red Shirt has a cleft in his chin. No — that's the boy in the blue shirt. What if they take off their shirts? How will I remember? O my God, these boys were going to ... *Count, Staceyann. Count!*

A large muscled arm wraps itself around my belly. Someone pulls at my navy blue bra. Breaks the strap. The left breast drops lower than the right. Red's hand snakes into my tank. The surprising smooth of his palm is silky on the loose breast. He *must* feel my heart jumping under his hand. Blue Shirt kisses my shoulder. Red Shirt presses his chest to my face.

Start counting, stupid — you will need the exact number later, later, when all of this is over.

The fleshy tongue fills my mouth. Red Stripe beer bitter on his breath. He was probably playing dominoes before he came in here. Beer and dominoes go together in Jamaica. I like dominoes. His lips behind my ear. I used to play dominoes with my cousins in Montego Bay. Stubble prickling my neck. We always played 'Cut Throat' every man for himself. No partners in here. I am playing by myself. Cut Throat. My body relaxes into the push and pull of the tug between them. Cut Throat. Wonder if I'll need therapy? But where does a lesbian get therapy in Jamaica?

Clumsy fingers struggle with the knot at my waist. The folds fall caressing at my feet.

I push Red's hands away from my panties. He slaps me open-palm across my face, bruises the inside of my lip. I taste the trickle of blood spreading over my tongue. Red Shirt is now directly in front of me.

I am going to need therapy. I can see my body in the shiny mirror above the sink. I look slimmer in this reflection, not so chunky in the waist. But why can't I look at their faces?

Fingers between my legs, I stand on tippy-toes to get away from the probing. They laugh when I do that. Red is in charge. His fingers explore the loose breast again, his hand thrusts me against the wet porcelain sink. The rough fabric of his shirt is itching my nose.

Everything goes dead when the large metal lock clicks. The door opens.

My heart races its relief when I turn to recognize Andrew. I had met him at one of those secret parties in the hills. He is one of us. He won't let them hurt me. It's over, now. It's over. Oh my God! Nothing really happened and it's all over! Thank you, Jesus! Thank you, Jesus.

I bend to pick up my sarong. Red grabs a hold of my right arm.

'Ease up, there, Baby-Love. Don't go nowhere, we soon come back to you.' Red turns to face Andrew.

'Alright, my youth. If you not for the cause, you must be against it. What you sayin? You leaving or you staying, with us or against us?'

Andrew pivots, as if to exit, and the lightning white rage bubbles up hot through the cistern of my constricted throat.

'Andrew, if you leave me here with them you won't live to see another sunrise!' The veiled threat jiggles my loose breast. Red fingers tighten around my arm. The little faggot is not going to leave me here! _He is going to help me!_

'You want me to tell you how I will do it?' I push my body against Red — to remind me that this is necessary, 'I will tell everybody where you go at nights and what…'

'What you want me to do?' He cuts me off. 'Me one can't fight all of them?'

I am almost sorry for him. But right now I need his consideration more than he needs mine.

'Andrew, if you leave me… '

'Alright, alright! I hear you the first time. I hear you the first time.'

'So, *Andrew*, why you don't want to join in? You is a batty bwoy or what? Free pussy and you refusin' — you must be a sodomite or a priest — and I don't see no Bible in you hand. Sonny bwoy, we beat faggot just fi fun, you know. Is mus bloodclaat batty you love! Is what you really sayin, you love man?'

'No, no, no … trust me, I love pussy just like the next man, but I don't like kill my own meat. I like it prepare and ready fi eat — ah mean ready fi fuck.'

'What that supposed to mean?'

'Well, we all civilized people, right? We a big man, now, right? Right. We get pussy all the time. It come to we — we no need fi run it down like ice-cream truck. Right?'

Red pushes me away from him and marches over to Andrew.

'Yow, don't feel is desperation make we have her in here, you know. We nah go fuck her because we can't get pussy — we trying to curb this lesbian business we hear bout her. We can't have them sodomite mongst we, free fi do all them nastiness. Make them feel is all good and well fi disrespect the way God put we down here fi live. Something have to be done bout this way of thinking that creeping on this island!'

Blue and White nod their agreement.

'Yes, man, we going fuck her to bring her back to the right way of thinking. We fucking her to save her from herself and from hellfire.'

'What if somebody find out? What if the police find out?' 'Who going tell them? You?'

'No, man, but just like I walk in here, somebody else can walk in too. Anybody can just walk in, the cleaning man, the plumber — anybody — and oonu say she a sodomite? What if she have some kinda fuck-up disease? What if she have AIDS?'

'The woman them get AIDS too?' Blue is visibly disturbed.

No one is holding me now. And I am five feet from the door. Five small steps.

'Yes, man, the whole a them fuck each other in them batty and all kinda nastiness — you never know, and them have some disease worse than AIDS.' Andrew is on a roll.

Four-and-a-half tiny feet to the door. Four-and-a-quarter. Four. All eyes are on Andrew.

'And you know, it quicker fi a man get AIDS from a woman than the other way around?'

Three-and-a-half feet. Sarong wrapped around my hips. Left hand holding the ends together.

Three feet.

'And more woman have AIDS than man. Some disease you can get just by touching…'

My right hand is two inches from the door. 'Where the Bloodclaat you think you going? Oonu hold her!'

That split second that no one wanted to touch me was all I needed to swing the door back and run. And run I did. Across the grass and down the seductive curve of Ring Road. Through the Arts parking lot. Blue cars. Red cars. White cars. Grass under my bare feet. Hot asphalt slapping the soles. Garden Boulevard, Violet Avenue, Begonia Drive. And then ... home.

When I come up gasping from that experience I decide it is time to consider America.

Memory, My City, My Home

HONOR FORD-SMITH

At the outset, I want to say how grateful I am to be in the company of writers and performers from the region and to be given the chance to talk among ourselves about our work in the Caribbean itself. Such events, sadly, are still rare despite the fact that Caribbean writing and publishing is blooming as never before. These contradictions continue to define the nature of the place I call home, a place marked by a mixture of old and intense social conflicts, lasting ancestral credit, energy grounded as a reggae bass line and a thick texture of memories whose images play and replay over and around me wherever I am.

The World in the City, the Past in the Present

How different would this writers' conference be if it were taking place elsewhere! How different if it were taking place downtown in Toronto or Brooklyn or Brixton — all Caribbean cities in their own way! Being together here in Kingston makes possible a consciousness of a debt to history that would be invisible, in the same way, elsewhere. Indeed, in the spirit of Walter Benjamin's much cited passage on the angel of history, I want to suggest that our presence here in this city of Kingston may also site us so that we are propelled into a future, albeit with our backs turned toward it,[1] a future already made mysterious by the debris of the wars of new empire.

With our faces turned to the past, we remember C.L.R. James's contention, that the Caribbean was the site of the first modern society in that earlier moment of globalization[2] even as we are blown into the vortex of the future. If we excavate the historical geologies of place, we find a pentimento of images that evoke a history of global interconnection based on imperial exchanges as violent as those of today. Those of us who have grown up on the surface of this geology fractured with unexpected cracks or layered with shifting sediments understand that while these old formations have made the world what it is and is not, they do not entirely constrain the conditions of possibility. Repetitious cycles of violence continue inter-generationally, but so too does something else, the stubborn and sometimes disorderly desire to create alternatives to it. It is that desire for an alternative that has become, for me, a reason for writing.

The foundational exchanges of fallen empires and their old colonies underlie the movements of people outside this room in a city marked by names that remind us of just who did what to whom and when. I am, for example, staying opposite Emancipation Park which is positioned on Oxford Road just off of Old Hope Road — Hope ironically being the name of a slave plantation which engulfed the plain the Tainos named for the iguana. I grew up on the Hope Road afraid of lizards and ignorant of the fact that the absence of Tainos meant the presence of the haunting shadow of genocide. I grew up diagonally opposite King's House where a stream of colonial governors and then Jamaican governors general came and went. One day, a Rasta man called Bob Marley moved into a house across the street. I watched as every afternoon he played football in the front yard. From there he released what he called 'redemption songs' or 'songs of freedom' which he said were 'all [he] ever had'; songs that changed popular music and disrupted stale representations of the African Diaspora forever. What a lesson in possibility!

For a time, I lived next door to the headquarters of the Palestinian Liberation Organization (PLO) in Jamaica. Known to most people as Arafat's Guest House, many claimed that the house at 55 Hope Road was a short stop hotel. The owner said he was Yassar Arafat's cousin. He often told the story of how he had fled Palestine, after his land was confiscated by Zionists. After years of guerilla activity, he settled into a more peaceful life in Kingston, naming his house after the leader of the PLO and telling the history of the occupation of Palestine to whomever he could make listen.

Next door to the PLO headquarters was Billy Boy's house. Yes, there really was such a person, and she lived at the corner of Hope and Lady Musgrave Road in an extraordinarily eccentric house which she won in a raffle on her return from a sojourn in Costa Rica where she seemed not to have made her fortune. The house had been built before I was born. It was raffled off by Gore's factory as a promotion for old man James Gore's entry into the local manufacturing industry. The colony was still almost entirely a plantation economy when Gore made his innovative move during World War II when boats could not move about freely and imports slowed. He seized the opportunity to manufacture brightly patterned tiles and ornamental concrete decorations for the local construction market. The house displayed and promoted his commodities. It flaunted every imaginable colour of glass and patterned tile and every concrete column and cement effigy from dwarfs to bearded grandsires in small, medium and large. Winning the house must have been the only lucky thing that ever happened to Billy for there she received the news that her niece and nephew had burned to death in the Gaiety fire. There her husband shot himself. (We children were told he was cleaning his gun). There Tottie used to fall in a trance frequently and unpredictably, her eyes turning over to that other invisible world where she received messages from the spirits while we children ran screaming into the arms of the plum tree.

That was where the wake for my cousin Turo was held. He belonged to a gang of light-skinned middle-class boys given to performing the role of the urban outlaw. The *Star* called them 'Sons of Gentry' and they were viewed as somewhat amusing, inauthentic, uptown imitations of the more roots rudie gangs emerging downtown. What motivated these privileged near-white youth to break houses and steal cars? What was wrong with these middle-class misfits who came from apparently unimpeachable respectability? What deep dissatisfaction made them do it? These questions were the topic of the conversations of those who sat on their cool grill-less St. Andrew verandahs in the 1960s chatting into the night. One night Turo and some friends ran a police roadblock (was it a stolen car? I can't remember). The police opened fire. Turo was hit and died quickly — a working-class death.

Now Billy Boy's house has been reinvented as Medallion Hall Hotel. On one side the hotel has swallowed up the empty lot beside it where she grew roses for the floral arrangements she made to earn her living. On the other side the hotel has swallowed up Arafat's guest house, the headquarters of the PLO, perhaps presaging the eclipse of Mr A. himself. Opposite, the shop and rum bar once run by Mr Chang is an American fast food chain called TGIF, and it does a roaring trade in fast food. The Hope Road itself has become a loud traffic jam, a soundscape of blowing horns, swearing drivers, child beggars and hustlers selling everything from reject roses, *Gleaner* and guinep to bodies and crack cocaine. This transformation has been made more rapid by the flight of businesses from downtown, presumably also a flight from payments of protection money, hustlers, beggars and gunfights. In due course all those who depend on the businesses must also relocate, so that I am forced to wonder where next the businessmen will flee.

Such intersections of the world in the city, the past in the present, make a kind of container in which my work moves back and forth. When I am able to engage with them, to borrow the novelist Vic Reid's phrase, they make noises in the blood and they echo in our bones. The body — as all actors know — is a place of knowing as well as a place of expression of that knowledge in performance. It is, as Diana Taylor might put it, both archive and repertoire.[3] If we allow ourselves the possibility of engaging with embodied memory, engaging with these echoes and those noises, we quickly become aware that our social, racial, spiritual and geographic positions make possible what we are able to know and how we know.

As a writer, I think it important to engage carefully with the ways in which we are positioned in this geology of time as well as in the global and local flow of bodies, labour, ideas and capital. Such an insight is hardly original. Indeed Sherene Razack, Trinidadian-Canadian scholar, has proposed that attentiveness to what we share and don't share in our different locations is critical to understanding not only the conditions of possibility around us but also how we might work together across difference.[4] It is also critical, I think, to how we position our interventions for that is what I think writing is — a form of cultural intervention or appeal to individuals who might change the way they think about policy, institutions of finance capital and governance, development and education, as well as the way they live their everyday lives. As Razack argues, attentiveness to our differences can be as important as our similarities for understanding the conditions of possibility in this new historical world. Mapping our places of entry into the world, understanding how that has formed us and made us who we are, can help us to understand the blind spots in our visions of possibility. Sketching the forces of power that form us and then working to understand how they deformed us can be a vital step to disrupting the violence that visibly and invisibly shapes our future.

I want to undertake just such an exercise, to trace how and where I entered as a performer and writer in this landscape and then to talk about the experiences that caused my work and my positioning to shift, analysing some of the things I think underlie those changes, pointing out how they have altered me.

Performing Love, Writing Loss

I never considered myself a writer, although writing was something I did. I thought of myself first and foremost as a performer and a teacher (and of course the two are related). Now I confine most of my performances to the classroom. But back then when I began my working life I thought of myself as an actress, and I remain concerned with directing, writing and teaching performance in all its many guises. My unremarkable debut took place at a family concert, perhaps in the Hope Road house. I don't remember it but I am told by family that I gave a rousing interpretation of that popular poem, 'The Owl and the Pussycat'. Unaware of all sexual innuendo,

I accompanied myself on a toy piano and bawled out the words loudly to the assembly. No doubt as I was only three my accompaniment did not have much to do with the conventional melody for the piece. There began my commitment to improvisation.

Perhaps it was at that moment that I learned that these performances made my mother smile. Pleasing her pleased me because it made me feel loved. It made me feel connected and grounded in community. This positive parental response has been the impulse for many a performer to thrust herself upon the world. In any case, performing seemed to me to open a space where I felt free — a space within which it was permissible to open up and express my feelings through the veil of a borrowed text. In a world riddled with secrets, taboos and strange rules about what was permissible and what was not, what could be said and what could not, I felt I had found a place to be spontaneous and I associated it with intimacy. At bedtime my mother and grandmother read to me, and I learned to listen and evaluate their performances as a part of the act of love and intimacy.

Writing, on the other hand, was quite a different matter. I have a slight dyslexia – which wasn't called that in the 1950s, when it was called laziness and failure to apply oneself. Early samples of my writing testify to the fact that I muddled up *b*'s and *d*'s, *h*'s and *y*'s and turned things upside down and backways. That I overcame this was entirely due to the instruction of a genius teacher at St. Hugh's Prep who I knew only as Miss Murray. She transformed letters and signs into metaphors and narratives. Adding was the business of a greedy man called Mr More who always wanted more and more, and subtraction was the business of a skinny man called Mr Less who was always losing things. *A* was a housetop and *B* had two big tummies while *D* had only one. Under the tutelage of Miss Murray we dressed up as nursery rhyme characters for pageants and plays in the school yard. She introduced us to Shakespeare and Macbeth by dressing up as a witch and jumping up and down around a bucket full of lollipops which she distributed as she recited:

Double, double toil and trouble;
Fire burn and cauldron bubble.[5]

There is something else though. Writing was fraught with conflict, because my earliest writing projects consisted of writing letters to my English father who after a violent divorce from my mother had gone back to England. He had been in the RAF in World War II and my Granny said he had something called shell shock. I didn't know what shell shock was, but I knew I had conflicting feelings about him. Nevertheless he was my father and these letters were the only way of maintaining a relationship with him and so I wrote them dutifully. While this epistolary relationship was probably less problematic than his living presence would have been, I did not know that at the time. I posted the letters and waited. The response would take months, sometimes years to come back. When it did come it was usually in the form of those old blue air letter forms which required great skill to open. I inevitably cut them open wrongly and they opened like wounded butterflies or dissected birds. I pieced them together painstakingly like a jigsaw puzzle, matching pieces of words and letters together across the fragmented paper. Sometimes I was successful and the message was decipherable. Sometimes whole fragments of the puzzle went missing.

From the start then writing and reading wasn't easy, even though I liked the feel of paper and pencil and enjoyed mimicking the power of those I saw seated at desks overflowing with papers in offices downtown. Writing was fraught with loss, haunted by violence and the conflict and difficulty of consciously cultivating a substitute for what I had lost — what Joseph Roach has called surrogation — a process by which you fill the cavities of loss with something else, always hoping to find the authentic original but producing something imprecise, marked only by its difference from the imagined original.[6] Writing was an attempt to make fading memory present, to bring it back to life through the jerky and faltering dialogue with an unknown but longed-for parent. And so what you wrote often bore no resemblance to what you felt or how you might have talked about the experience if you hadn't been tethered to a memory of something that ought to have been but wasn't. Writing was all the time about longing and loss, but never the fulfilment of satisfaction.

The problem deepened when we went to high school and one of our teachers told us that we should not attempt to write poetry or fiction on the O-level exam because only the most deeply sensitive imaginative beings could write literature. Writers, she said, were more sensitive than anyone else. We on the other hand were not sensitive and should confine ourselves to writing essays, if we wished to pass the exam. And it seemed clear that if you wanted to be a writer you had to be born in Britain or France or Spain before the twentieth century.

Performance became a way around all of this. It was the thing I did easily, was not examined on by Cambridge or any other legitimating institution, was rewarded for and loved for immediately, and that became my work. I enjoyed most creating in improvisation, which seemed to me to be a process of writing with the body. It was a way of laying out signs in much the same way as writing involves laying out alphabetic signs. With performance you laid them out with your body in front of an audience who decoded the signs and signalled back to you right away what they understood. It was immediate. It was sweaty. It was embodied. It was collaborative.

For years I worked at what is now the Edna Manley College and at the Sistren office at 100 Hope Road and then Kensington Crescent in what was a quintessentially postcolonial moment. When I joined the staff at the Jamaica School of Drama to work with Carroll Dawes, Dennis Scott, Hertencer Lindsay, Rawle Gibbons, Henry Muttoo and others, our work was all about creating regional and national identity for, far from emerging naturally from our environment, the way we imagined this community and its possibility had to be constructed and taught. The task at hand in this early period after political independence was decolonization, the inventorying of what Edward Said called the cultural reserve, rewriting the colonial narrative of history, creating heroes and heroines from outlaws and acts of resistance, working toward the creating of a new postcolonial subject in education.[7] Since we all live according to the stories we are told and are inspired by those stories to change the conditions of our lives, our task as teachers/artists was to create new narratives of identity and community. Performance became a site for the production of knowledge about who 'we' were. Of course there were arguments and conflicts and differences about the limits of this 'we': who was in and who out, who was on top and who on the bottom or in the middle and, as Walcott and Scott pointed out long before the theorists of Cultural Studies, our notions of self depended in a contradictory way on stable ideas of the other — who was more often than not the colonizer. In spite of this there was little other possibility than to begin to inventory difference from dominant identity. While there were heated disputes around religion, language, race, gender, and around class and sexuality, essentially our small team shared a commitment to developing cultural narratives of identity and to building a pedagogy of citizenship.

Neoliberalism, Violence and the Re-organization of Identity

I think you know the rest of the story. The cold war ended and the hot one began. The IMF hurricane hit. Hundreds of budget cuts later, we came face to face with the fact that postcolonialism was not so post and that the world had entered a new phase of globalization in which everything can be reduced to a market relation, commodified, circulated, exchanged and consumed. Indeed the key basis of neoliberalism is that market exchange becomes an ethic in itself and a guide for human action.[8] Anything that cannot be commodified is worthless. As the tentacles of expanding commodification reach out, borders of poor countries are forced open, labour is devalued and industry re-organized across borders, torpedoing small-scale national economies, wiping out local food production and torpedoing the dream of the likes of Mr James Gore for a manufacturing sector that serves a local market.

I do not want to suggest simplistically that the present order offers only banal domination. The picture is of course much more complicated than that. But it has taken a long time for the dust to clear enough for the possibilities to be apprehended. The process of transformation of the globe is horrible and it is also a tremendous moment of opportunity. New forms of economy and governance suggest new forms of resistance and new possibilities for transformation. My focus today is less on possibility than it is on the violence that has accompanied this global reorganization and its implications for cultural work.

To be effective, power has to perform its narratives, as James Scott has argued.[9] These diverse performances have ranged from countless American invasions (Haiti, Grenada and Panama, to name a few in our region) to the militarization of cities through security companies, the police, and armed 'posses' which have become signatures of the city of Kingston, as they have in Medellin, Rio and elsewhere. The entry of Jamaica, and more specifically Kingston, into this new global order has been marked by a violence that cannot be explained simply as the playing out of a local problem. It is part of a pattern of violence which has marked the racialized re-organization of the globe, the opening of some borders, the lockdown of others, the jettisoning of capital investment in some places and its landing in others, and the consequent movement of millions of bodies as a result of this. This violence has been performed in different ways in the Americas and with different consequences. In Argentina, it was played out in the drama of the disappeared under the military dictatorship. Thirty thousand people were murdered in that dirty war. In Colombia the script is of wars between the army, the paramilitaries, the guerillas and the coca lords. In Nicaragua and El Salvador violence played out in formal civil wars which gave way to informal civil violence. In each case, as in the case of Jamaica, violence has built on the legacies of the cold war, violent destabilization of left-leaning regimes and the reorganization of consumption, industry, food production and land use.

In each case, localized myths, images and explanatory narratives that folks held about themselves have been exploded, re-organized and sold back to us in new packages through the re-organized networks of global and local communication and finance. In other words, neoliberalism is accompanied by a dramatic, often forced transformation of identity — at both an individual and a collective level. Violence is the force that brings about this transformation. Every one of us from this city has tales to tell about the violence of the life of the city. Every one of us can see the way it has transformed the architecture of the city, and we can recount the ways it has transformed who we think we are. The consequences are of course unevenly shared. The brunt of the agony is borne by working-class communities, where the death toll and the mutilation is highest. But it has consequences for middle-class communities too. For me, my relationship with Death, the Don Gorgon, changed my relationship to my work and pushed me toward a more major shift in the themes that preoccupy me. I have written extensively about the death of my mother in the poetry collection *My Mother's Last Dance*. Today I want to tell the story of another encounter with death.

The Messiah of Stony Hill

After I left home I lived for many years in a place called Tree Tops in Stony Hill. The first time I saw the place I thought it incredibly beautiful. It was a simple concrete three-story building that looked out on Pigeon Valley. It balanced on the edge of a steep cliff of white rock like a lighthouse. It was surrounded by poinciana trees and elephant ear vines. It had moss-covered courtyards, night blooming jasmine, ginger lilies and wild banana and there were birds everywhere.

Tree Tops belonged to Marcus, who was my landlord for about ten years. He was tall, dark and handsome — and mad as shad. Or so I thought anyway. He had been educated at Kingston College and then joined the RAF, like my father, becoming a pilot in World War II. He had done many missions in Germany before being sent on the most dangerous of all missions, the bombing of Berlin. He told me that when he flew into Berlin the sky would be lit up with a million lights like fireworks. 'Why did they have fireworks during the war, Marcus?' I asked. 'Shrapnel, you idiot!' he snapped.

One night when he was returning to base from a successful mission he looked out of the plane and caught the eye of the German pilot who was about to blow him out of the sky. He baled out fast and parachuted down.

He landed somewhere in Holland where the Dutch Resistance found him. They said they couldn't hide him because he was too black. He'd give them away. Soon the Germans found him and he became a prisoner of war in a camp somewhere near the border of Poland and Russia. 'I was the only black man in the camp,' he told me. 'I took up boxing and became camp champion. I was a mascot for them, I suppose. No complaints! RAF prisoners were extremely well treated.'

Toward the end of the war when the Nazis began to lose, the Red Cross couldn't get through the lines and the prisoners had nothing to eat. They were ravenous. That was when Marcus began having visions. Once he saw Hitler and Goering enter his barracks. He picked them up on his little finger and threw them into the air. They floated down slowly and landed on the tip of his little finger. That was when he knew he was the Messiah.

He confided this to me one day when he was helping me repaint the apartment that I shared with my friend Hilary.

'Well Marcus, if you are the Messiah you shouldn't be concerned about worldly things like rent. You should let us all live here free.'

'That's why I don't like to tell people,' he grumbled. 'Nobody understands.'

I had annoyed him, interrupted his narrative, and I never did find out any more about the camp or how he got to England where he had lived for many years or how he met his English wife — whose bright red hair dye he borrowed from time to time. Years later, my neighbour told me that Marcus had done a forced march to Berlin at the end of the war when the Germans retreated. He had walked for miles across the European countryside and city without shoes or warmth or food until they reached Berlin.

At Tree Tops Marcus painted pictures all the time. His favourite themes were religious or sexual and he wasn't partial about where he painted them. He painted on bagasse board, an invention of the 1970s that seems to have become extinct. He painted on the glass jalousies. He painted on plywood. He painted on the garage door. He ate very little, smoked lots of ganja, drank tea up on the roof. He invented new spiritual mythologies for the hillside. Mrs Hanna who lived across the road was the reincarnation of Nefertiti, he said. Somebody else was Venus, but I forget who. In my essence I was a heart attired in the paraphernalia of a hen. Jamaica was a little pig lying on its side and Marcus Garvey was god made man. Quetzalcoatl, the bird/god of the Mexicans, was a frequent visitor to Tree Tops, Marcus said. Apparently he found sanctuary in Pigeon Valley after the invasion of what is now Mexico by the Spanish. 'He dangles his wonderful member over the roof because it so close to the skies. Then he disappears,' Marcus informed me one morning after such a visit as I was on my way out to work. Sometimes he would send written versions of his vision to me. He rolled them up, tied them with a piece of string and lowered them in the direction of the lowest flat where I lived. I would find them dangling outside my window.

Every Easter Marcus said he battled with Satan. I became involved in one of these battles, he told me, when I gave birth to a spirit at the foot of his bed. The spirit went into him and made him luminous to his bones, causing the devil to depart but not without a parting last lick which left a bloody mark on his forehead.

As far as I knew Marcus had little more than his stories and his paintings. I knew that I received the sum of about ten pounds a year for a period of ten years from the British Government for the sacrifice of my father's sanity for king and country. Marcus couldn't have got much more, if that. He lived on our rent — mine and Hilary's. And that was all of $600 — very little even 20 years ago.

I was afraid of Marcus. I have always been afraid of madness and I thought him mad. This of course was because I was afraid of the possibility of madness in myself. Madness they said had been my father's problem and I closely resembled him didn't I? No one said so directly, but then they didn't have to. In a thousand ways they made it obvious that they feared I might inherit his madness or his badness, depending on which family member's interpretation you preferred. I certainly was quite different from the majority of my family, who were down to earth and hardworking and who, with the exception of my mother, mistrusted artists and claimed that too much education resulted in impractical and irritating excesses of intellect that could possibly buss yuh brain. I didn't know then that, regardless of genetics, this fear of madness and unconventionality was fear of a colonial stereotype of near-white West Indians. I should have known, for I had read *Jane Eyre*, but I had perhaps chosen not to absorb this message.

One night in 1985, the new Sistren Headquarters on Kensington Crescent was opened by Lucille Mathurin Mair. I remember that there wasn't enough curry goat to go around and that Bello (Winston Bell) appeared in an Actor Boy costume, saying he thought it appropriate to wear a dress, that the steelband from UWI played in the yard, and that women from the construction collective led a road march around the block chanting 'The communists are coming! The communists are coming!' I drank too much rum punch. After I dropped off folks around the city, Hilary and I got back to Tree Tops at about 1:00 a.m. I stumbled up the stairs and fell into deep rum-induced sleep immediately.

I woke up to a terrible noise. It was still dark and it sounded as if somebody was hurling a huge mahogany wardrobe across the room. I wondered why anyone would want to change their furniture around in the middle of the night. And then I thought 'Marcus is beating his wife.' But it was not his practice to beat his wife. Perhaps if I had drunk less rum punch I would have come to my senses quicker. It finally registered that there was one hell of a fight going on over my head. I ran into the living room, grabbed the phone which had a long chord and banged on Hilary's door en route. She'd also been awakened by the noise. We locked ourselves in my room at the back of the flat. The phone was still working and we argued about what to do. We screamed uselessly into the darkened valley. I called a neighbour who sounded annoyed and hung up rudely. I called the police, yelling into the phone 'Come, come now! Somebody is being murdered!' To my annoyance they wanted details like our address and how to get there. As I gave it, I gravely realized they wouldn't find their way up the mountain road for a long time. It was another neighbour, George Campbell, the cousin of an old school friend, who rescued us. We called him as a last resort after the police. He hardly knew us but he jumped out of his bed and came immediately. I remember he called to us from across the valley. 'I am here and I am armed. I've spoken to the police and they're nearby, but lost. I am going to get them. Don't move till I come.' When they got to us and we were able to unlock the door and come out, Marcus was unconscious, a long limp body being stuffed into the back of the police jeep to be taken to Emergency. The ambulance was lost. We hadn't heard the gun go off. It had a silencer, they said. I looked at George's gun. It resembled an elegant cigarette lighter.

The gunmen — gun children really — had come in through the windows of the top floor, the floor closest to the road, the windows Marcus had refused to grill. They had made their way downward through the house which had one central staircase. They demanded money and ransacked the place. When they threatened to tie up Marcus and rape his wife in front of their two-year-old grandchild, he decided he'd had enough. He attacked them unarmed. They shot him in the spine, paralysing him completely, and then gun-butted him mercilessly. At the hospital he lingered for a few months and then died.

I left Tree Tops the next day and returned to my mother's house on Hope Road. I abandoned Hilary who had no family in Jamaica and I abandoned the place I had loved. The house on Hope Road seemed unassailably safe. But there was to be no safety anywhere. Two weeks later my mother was hit off the Palisadoes road by a man in a rent-a-car. Both she and Marcus ended up on clean flour bag sheets at different ends of the orthopedic ward of the University Hospital. Marcus gave me one of his flowers to take across to her and sent a message of courage and hope.

It took me a long time to figure out that Marcus had likely saved all our lives. It struck me that he had fulfilled his own vision of who he was — the Messiah of Stony Hill. Marcus said that one of the gunmen had the face of a young demon. So he had died in one of his fights with the devil, only at Christmas rather than Easter. The lone survivor of a war time mission, blasted out of the skies over Europe in World War II, had survived prison camp and forced march to be finished off quickly by two thieves in a suburb of Kingston.

I had no way of explaining what had happened to me. I had only a list of unanswerable questions. Why had this hermit, this isolated self-taught artist and ascetic, likely the poorest person on Gibson Road, been attacked in this way? No justice there. And what had transformed the young gunman into Marcus's demon? And where was the devil who had masterminded the demonic transformation? Where were those who anonymously created an evil so banal, so ordinary, that children became absorbed into it as easily as they breathed the air around them? Where were those faceless ones who had created the conditions that made children kill for absolutely nothing? I had no way of understanding what had taken place or explaining how it coincided with the fact that my mother was going to die. I knew that, compared to those who had lost their children or other loved ones in violence, my tribulation was trivial, but it was mine, and I knew I was losing my family, community and the ground I called home.

Survivors of violence begin by denying its effects. A wilful amnesia is necessary if you are to go on. You have to deny the aftershocks, suppress the rage, displace the depression, the flood of memories triggered by a car backfiring, or a door slamming. You have to forget in order to live, but, as studies of trauma show, in forgetting you give in to terror and initiate an endless intergenerational cyclical violence.

That was when my work began to change. A peck on the cheek from the Don Death is an excellent way to check your priorities and get them in order. And so I began to put mine in order. I didn't want to lose my home as I had known it. It wasn't perfect but it was all I had. And I wanted my home to be a place of safety. I didn't want to forget those who risk their lives for love. And I didn't want to forget those who, having nothing to risk, risked their lives for nothing. Or those who achieved identity only by pumping lead into somebody or tearing flesh from limb.

Writing became my way of confronting, reconstituting and questioning what was being killed off and what was being born. Everywhere, bodies were crumbling around me. Everywhere, bodies displayed their fragility. Bodies full of holes, body parts missing or twisted. For the first time I couldn't speak through the masks of other characters, other lives, and I couldn't risk improvisation because it wasn't safe. That trusting audience had run for cover. I had to remember. To forget is to bow to violence's power. To forget is to be caught without escape in that underground labyrinth of easy familiar repetitive violence that long ago deformed and gave birth to the landscape we live in. To remember is to represent the cost of violence as it is. Unglamorous scar tissue. Pock-marked half lives. A tedious melodrama of victim and perpetrator that repeats and repeats. To remember is to begin to strip off the cloak of denial and face the power that produces young men who kill for nothing because there is nothing else.

In this changing city, historical sediments of older forms of violence mingle with the vulgar wars of the new global order. Patterns of violence are familiar to us. They echo in our bones, make noises in our blood. Writing against these new wars which turn poor people against each other is one way to cross the borders dividing our city into us and them. It is one way to address the crumbling architecture of our city and re-create the stubborn desire for an alternative to repetitive cyclical sounds of gunfire echoing across the changing imperial order.

Notes

1. Benjamin, cited in C. Forche, *The Angel of History* (New York: HarperCollins, 1994).
2. C.L.R. James, *The Black Jacobins* (New York: Vintage,1989).
3. D. Taylor, *The Archive and the Repertoire: Performing Cultural Memory in the Americas* (Durham, North Carolina: Duke University Press, 2003).
4. S. Razack, 'Your place or mine? Transnational feminist collaboration', in *Anti Racist Feminism: Critical Race and Gender Studies*, eds. A. Calliste and George J. Sefa Dei (Halifax: Fernwood Publishing, 2000).
5. William Shakespeare, *Macbeth* (Cambridge: Cambridge University Press, 1993), Act IV, Sc.1.
6. Joseph Roach, *Cities of the Dead: Circum-Atlantic Performance* (New York: Columbia University Press, 1996).
7. E. Said, *Culture and Imperialism* (New York: Random House, 1994).
8. D. Harvey, *The New Imperialism* (Oxford: Oxford University Press, 2003); A. Ong, *Neoliberalism as Exception: Mutations in Citizenship and Sovereignty* (Durham: Duke University Press, 2006).
9. J. Scott, *Domination and the Arts of Resistance: Hidden Transcripts* (New Haven: Yale University Press, 1990).

A State of Being

JEAN SMALL

It is not a matter of saying to yourself that you have attended a few writing workshops, that you've had some outrageously painful life experiences, that you know your life story inside out, and now you're going to write a helluva bestseller. That's not how it happens.

It may happen that you are having a conversation with a sister, an intimate conversation, as sisters are likely to have, the type of intimate conversation that's difficult to have with a brother or even a husband. You're talking about something topical, like incest or rape. (These are always topical in Jamaica.) And in the middle of the conversation you remember an incident that took place a long time ago when you were a little girl in British Guiana.

You tell the sister that your mother used to let you go to matinée every Saturday afternoon to see Shirley Temple movies and you had already become fascinated by the world of acting and actors. So one day after school you stop by the Rialto cinema (on Vlissengen Road) to gaze at the posters of your favourite film stars. It's two o'clock in the afternoon. There's no one at the front of the cinema. It's deathly quiet. And while you are in your private reverie a man who works at the cinema approaches you and asks, 'Yuh eva see de room weh dey show de movies?' Of course you hadn't. Nor had anyone in your class. This was going to be a real adventure. So, excitedly, you let him take you to the back of the building, up the stairs, into the room where they showed the movies. And you are innocently admiring everything in the room that can magically take you to other lands, other places and even make you feel like a black Shirley Temple. You turn around to thank him and _(primal scream)_[1] he has already dropped his pants and exposed a 'gody'.[2] Big swollen testicles. Red! Frightened, you bolt out of the room and you run and run and run down the road home, never to tell your mother, never to tell anyone, never to recall that incident until you are about 55 or so having an intimate conversation with a sister. It's just something that happened when you were a child. Long ago! You're not embarrassed to speak about it because in fact you were not raped. It happened a long time ago. It's not important. But the sister (Betty Wilson) is moved and she says to you, 'You know, you should write these things down.'

And so, one day, you begin to write, and as you write you see those swollen testicles again. Red! You realize that that image had never left you. You suddenly begin to understand why at age 55 or so, you are having problems having sex. You begin to understand why when you're about to 'do it' you find it difficult to look at the penis; why when you are about to 'do it' the light must be turned off. And suddenly it doesn't upset you anymore that he says you don't know how to do it, or that you're frigid, or that you are so ugly, so physically unattractive, so unintelligent, and that something is wrong with you because you're not like Shirley or Betty or Yvonne. It doesn't matter anymore because at age 55 or so you are beginning to understand why you are the way you are, that the trauma of that incident a long time ago had made an indelible mark on your personality, your emotions, your reactions to people and circumstances. You suddenly have a tremendous sense of ownership of who you are. It is empowering. It gives you a marvelous sense of control. It is even exciting and nothing else matters. This is such a personal triumph of self-discovery that you want to help others to do the same. You suddenly have a reason to write.

But you recall that every story needs a premise and you discover you have one: _the marking experiences in your life make you what you are._ Having defined the premise you feel ready to write. You wonder if this is how Trevor Rhone felt when he decided to write _Bellas Gate Boy_, his

autobiographical one-person play. You try unsuccessfully for three months
to get an interview with the busy writer, and then you remember that in a
radio interview with you he had spoken about this very point:

Recorded excerpt from an interview with Trevor Rhone[3]

JS: I think the wonderful thing about *Bellas Gate Boy* is that you didn't deny your past. Some people like to hide their early beginnings.

TR: My past is such an integral part of my existence and of the person that I am that it's very dear to me. No, I could never deny my past.

JS: So many people in the Caribbean have started from humble beginnings and gone to great heights.

TR: We've nearly all started somewhere way below the poverty line.… I think one of the critical things, Jean, is nowadays lots of doors and windows and apertures have been opened and young people today can at least see that it's possible. People of my generation had no models at all. There was nobody you knew who had walked through that door before.

JS: And the interesting thing is that you had the belief and the desire and the passion to get there even though the models weren't there. Something in your head made you want to get there.

TR: That's the essential difference between then and now.

JS: Some of our musicians were like that. Starting to play the guitar on a sardine tin with a string. Why is it that they kept this dream to get there even in the face of tremendous tremendous odds and need and lack of money and inspiration from people around them?

TR: I have a theory about that Jean. Some of us are blessed and lucky enough to have been chosen by some God or gods or some special person, just to take a message to the community around us. First of all to the immediate community and then sometimes to the community at large, and no matter what the obstacles are those people have to find a way.

All of you creative writers here know that to create a character you have to do the research on their background. The past, as Rhone said, is an essential part of character. You cannot write the life of anyone if you don't understand that writing is 'having a personal affiliation to the material' (Clifford Odets).[4] If you are going to write the life of Miss Ida — living in a one-bedroom in Kintyre with a leaking roof, who sleeps with a tarpaulin by her side to cover herself when the rain falls, who has to get up and walk down a rocky road to go and do her day's work — you have to get into the skin of Miss Ida. This was the challenge for Makeda Solomon as she prepared to perform in the one-woman show _A Song for Lena_. Makeda told me that she was fascinated by the story of this black woman and in order to create the character she went in search of more details. She read the court transcripts, she looked at pictures of Lena in prison (which made her more 'real' to her), and she watched movies of the Deep South to understand the social context and to assist with mastering the accent, the body language, the mannerisms so that she could find a way to add her voice in transporting Lena to the audience.

A one-person play is not a monologue. For a one-person play to be called a play there must be a cast of characters that the one person performs. In playing Trevor Rhone in _Bellas Gate Boy_, Alwyn Scott focused less on Rhone and more on playing the other characters in his life as seen and experienced by Rhone. I think that is why he was able to play all those characters and find all the voices so convincingly. You have to know what Odets calls the 'psychological gallery' of people in the life of the character, and you have to become those characters to find their voices and their mannerisms. Similarly, to begin to write creatively you have to place yourself in 'a state of being' the character. I take the term from the American playwright Clifford Odets who speaks about the difference between a very skilled writer, whom he describes as a craftsman not unlike the carpenter who with his nails and hammer could skilfully build anything, and the creative writer who starts with himself — something inside of himself. He doesn't start outside of himself. He doesn't just pick a form and decide to write a bestseller. The form is dictated by the material.

So you make a collection of the most traumatic moments in your life. In your particular case it is not finding the many influential people in your life, it is finding the many changed persons you are at different stages of your life and the marking experiences that caused the changes. And so you document your life experiences from the time you were a pre-teen to a teenager, an adult and your understanding of those various traumatic moments allows you to even go beyond yourself and imagine someone like yourself responding in a way that you now expect that character to respond so the character is you, but is not you, but could possibly be you. And when you go even further to extend yourself into the future and see yourself as an old lady going back in time and remembering your life and telling the story of your life like 'gang-gang'[5] storytelling. And people ask you why did you make the old lady go mad in the end. It is because when people re-member these traumatic moments of their lives, the pain of remembering can make them go temporarily mad. And when people ask you why you made the old lady tell her life's experiences in French, it is because you know that the old storyteller goes back in time and remembers in his/her maternal language which is usually a creole. But since you do not have creole as your maternal language you tell it in French which is your other language and which provides the linguistic mask you need in recounting a painful experience.

So you have documented the series of marking experiences and you have to tell them because you want to share the discovery of self. What form should you use? You have dabbled in theatre and so you are already visualizing the characters in your head as you write. You are confident that you can re-enact them and that the quickest way to communicate your story is through performance on stage. You begin to choose the experiences that you think you can bring alive by performance. You decide to tell your story in the form of a play, a one-person play. You have no money to hire a theatre to rehearse, but you discover that you are capable of sitting in a chair, of closing your eyes and imagining the space in which you will tell your story. And as you imagine the space you work out the blocking in your head. You learn to turn your eyes in on yourself and see the whole performance before you have done it. This is another exciting discovery.

Then you have to create the language for each you at different stages. To do this you have to strip yourself of the present and go back in time to get into the skin of yourself at a point in the past, find the body language and the voice. You become that pre-teen again. You remember your orphaned friend in primary school. You play her and you are not her. You are really you because, at the time of writing, you have become orphaned so you understand what it feels like to be an orphan, and you cry because it is her, it is you, and it is all of us displaced orphans ripped from the shores of Africa and brought to the Caribbean.

(At this point you remove your dress, strip yourself of earrings, watch, spectacles and, dressed in a primary school uniform complete with shoes and socks and a black wig parted in two and tied with ribbons, you descend from the podium to the front of the audience and demonstrate in performance how one gets into the skin of a character assuming the voice and mannerisms of a pre-teen child. In the voice of the child you continue to explain the process.)

> Wen I waz in primary school my bes frien waz a orphan … an … an … wen I become my frien…. I waz a orphan too … but den I tink ov all de Africans slaves … dat … dat … come here an how dey waz made orphans too … an so wen I cry iz becoz I trying to mek a tri … tri … triplo … tripli … triplicate de orphan. An yuh see wen I went to England … an I do my play … an a white lady she come an cry… becoz she feel it … den iz wen I know dat wen yoh get in de state ov being de character … it does be au … au … thentic. An yuh see … wen yuh get in dis state ov being it does become so real … dat it tek a long time to come out ov it.

(You then very slowly come out of the character, to be yourself and end the presentation.)

Notes

1. Prof Rex Nettleford suggested that each traumatic moment should be expressed in the form of a primal scream.

2. A 'gody' is a Guyanese word for swollen testicles due to a rupture. See Richard Allsopp, *Dictionary of Caribbean English* (Oxford: Oxford University Press, 1996).

3. Interview done in 2005 at the then Radio Mona, UWI for the series *A Festival of Words* produced and hosted by Jean Small. Alwyn Scott was also interviewed for this programme.

4. Clifford Odets interviewed by Arthur Wagner, *The Lincoln Theatre Review* 42 (Spring 2006). Many of the theories expressed by Odets coincide exactly with my own process.

5. 'Gang-gang' is a term used in Jamaican creole for the old grandmother or 'nana' who passes on wisdom in the form of stories.

Carnival Is Marse

PAUL KEENS-DOUGLAS

Yu know, plenty people like to feel dat because yu come from Trinidad, yu suppose to be able to dance, yu suppose to like Pelau an dem kind ah ting, an yu suppose to like Calypso an be able to sing it too. Dey cant understand when ah man say he dont play Carnival. 'Someting got to be wrong wit he, he not from here, where he come from?' But yu see, some people born to play, an some people born to 'spectate', to look on.

Well I tink I am ah born spectator, because I not lucky wit carnival band at all, at all. I have ah history of bad luck wit carnival band. De first band I ever play wit in my life, was ah band call 'De Horrors of Dracula.' Well, was real horrors. Was ah 'Small Band,' ah real small, band, ah mean de band was so small, de whole side went to de Savannah in ah taxi. Dat was ah 'small band.' If you see us dress-up like dis Dracula, one set ah black clothes, an cape all down to de ground. An if you see false teet in we mout. One Dr Watts make de false teet for we. Man only keep bitin deyself. When we cross de stage, nobody was quite sure what we was. Our band was de only band ever win 'Individual of de Year.'

An we put on big act yu know. I had on ah raincoat over me costume, an de rest of de band was suppose to surround me on stage like dey bitin me, an I had was to take off de raincoat, an come out in me costume like I turn ah Dracula. An ah fella was suppose to drop some ole bones on de ground to represent my body. Only problem was, he couldnt get no human bones; so he gone by de butcher an get some ole cow head, an pig foot, an sheep ribs, an tings like dat, an is dat de man put on de stage. Well, yu could imagine laugh. If dey had ah comedy prize we would ah sure win dat. After dat, ah tell dem not me an Carnival, ah say it must have more to Carnival dan dat.

De nex year dey come an tell me how de mistake ah make was goin an play in ah Small Band. Dey say, 'Boy, yu play de wrong ting, join ah Medium Size Band, Small Band is for little boys, Medium Size Band is for big man!' Den dey tell me how dey playin something call 'De Glories Dat Was Greece.' Dey tell me how I goin to be ah Roman Emperor, den dey tell me ah should try for someting ah little bigger, so I end up as 'Mars — The God of War.'

Well, de costume wasnt too bad, but de problem was de helmet. Yu see in those days, yu didnt buy nothin, yu had to make it yuself. An if you wasnt too artistic, an couldnt make yu own helmet, yu had to get somebody to make it for yu. Well, de fella who make my helmet was either Cokey-eye, or else he was blind in one eye an cant see in de next one. If yu see de helmet. De front like it vex wit de back. De front gone so, an de back gone so. When ah put it on, ah look as if ah have ah bolt of lightning on top me head. Ah had headache for bout ten years after dat. Ah say it must have more to Carnival dan dat.

Den one day a fella come an tell me, 'Forget dem amateurs, if yu want to play real mas, play wit ah professional.' He tell me play wit Saldenah, dat is ah real Mas-man! So poor me go an sign up wit Sally. Dat year Sally play 'Ah Sailor Is Ah Sailor' — I was ah 'Drunken Sailor'. De only section ah could get in. Ah eh know nobody in de section. Yu ever play in ah section an yu eh know nobody in it? Den dey tell me how my section comin out from Diego-Martin, to go down dey early Carnival Monday mornin an collect me costume.

So I gone down dey Carnival Monday mornin. When ah ask for me costume, ah lil skinny fella tell me wait, an he gone in de back. Well he gone so long, ah say dey mus be now sewin it. Nex ting ah see ah fella comin wit someting dat look like ah engagement ring box. My costume was in dat. Five hundred dollars wort of costume, in ah Engagement Ring box.

An if you see costume. De fella who shop for Sally, like he buy everyting de same size. Ah had purple bell-bottom pants. If you see dem. Three foot in front, three foot behind. When ah do so, me foot lookin like ah axe. Like de man who buy for Sally didnt know nothin bout size in trut. We had ah white tank-top vest bout five size too small. When ah put it on, it cant go inside me pants at all, at all. So ah had to bend over, push it in my waist, an stay so for de whole day. If ah ever do so, tank-top flyin up an hit me in me nose.

As for de hat an dem, well he buy all hat de same size, size three. Was ah white sailor hat, three sizes too small. It couldnt even go over me forehead. When ah put it on, ah look like ah tube ah Colgate toothpaste. But de gloves was de best. We had some white gloves, bout ten size too small. When ah put dem on, dey could hardly go on, first dey tight. Ah had to bend all me fingers, an keep dem bend like dat, if ah ever do so. . . gloves gone.

So see me Carnival Monday now, jumpin up, tank-top stick inside me pants here, me body bend like ah safety-pin to keep it dey, hat turn inside-out on top me head to make it fit me, an me two hands curl up like claws to make sure de gloves stay on, an ah jumpin up like dat for de whole day. People only sayin, 'Poor fella, ah wonder if he born so or he was in ah accident?' Ah say it must have more to Carnival dan dat.

Den dey come an tell me how ah play wit de wrong professional. De say, 'Boy, what yu really have to do is go an play with Edmond Hart!' Dey say dat is band, he does play for fun, yu go enjoy yuself, plenty woman, nakedness, 'yu go enjoy yuself, nice band!' Ah go an sign up wit Edmond Hart. Dat year Edmond play someting call 'Tribute to Broadway'. De only section I could get into was ah section call Mary Poppins. Dey tell me how I am a Chimney Sweep.

If you see de costume. Ah red an white stripe pants. When ah put it on ah look like ah wukkin Royal Castle sellin chicken. An den button hole here, button over dey. When ah button-up, ah twist like dat, like ah piece ah wire. Den dey put ah tank-top on me, tie ah long scarf wrap round me neck, like dey want to choke me to death, put ah red hat on me head, gimme ah broomstick, two white gloves, charge me bout four hundred dollars, an tell me I am ah Chimney Sweep in Mary Poppins.

Den ah have to walk by meself from Cascade to Belmont to meet de band. Yu ever walk by yuself, in yu costume, in de middle of de road, on ah Carnival Monday? Embarrassin! Taxi stoppin, 'Wha is dat he playin?' Little children callin yu, 'Mama watch ah mas passin!' People wavin at yu. 'Boy, wha yu playin? Wha band yu from? Yu band loss?' All kinda ting. Embarrassin! Now I know why people does take car to go an meet dey band. Everybody fraid to walk by deyself in dey costume. Ah say it must have more to Carnival dan dat.

De nex year now, dey tell me forget band, save yu money, forget Tuesday Mas, concentrate on havin ah good time, an de best time to do dat is J'Ouvert. An de ting to do, is to go an jump up wit Invaders, after dat yu dont have to do nutten, jus go home an sleep, Invaders is de ting. Ah ask dem where Invaders comin out from. Dey tell me go up Tragarete Road ah go see plenty people walkin round lookin like dey loss, dat is where Invaders is. So ah go up dey, an ah see bout ten thousan people lookin loss, ah say right, dat is where Invaders is.

Yu ever jump up wit Invaders on ah J'Ouvert mornin? Is ah art. Dem specialize in slowness. We leave bout four o'clock de mornin, ah reach Independence Square aroun ten, meet de other bands goin back, we now reach down dey. An everybody who jumpin wit Invaders is like dey know everybody else. If you hear dem. Dey jumpin up an carryin on big conversation. 'How de wife? Children in school yet?', 'Yu have visitors dis year?', 'Ah forget de stove on, but ah eh goin back at all, de house could burn down!', 'You is Mr Johnson daughter, ah eh see de family for a long time. How yu mudder? She dead? How yu father? He dead too? How yu sister? She dead too? Ae, ae, all ah allyu dead, wha happen, you dead too?'

An while dis conversationisation takin place, everybody tryin to jump up near de band to get de sweet music. An de panmen like dey feel dem people eh have deodorant, dey dont want dem near dem at all. Dey pushin de pan thru de crowd like is lawnmower dey have, an people scatterin left, right, an centre, but dey still dey wit de band. Ah nearly break me foot bout six time near Laperouse Cemetery, ah pan run over me heel, me foot go down in pothole, in manhole, if yu see me, jumpin over drain, jumpin over box, jumpin over bottle. Ah spend de whole J'Ouvert mornin tryin not to go in hospital. Half dem people yu see jumpin high so, is not de music have dem so yu know, is dey bigtoe dey tryin to save. But dey still wit Invaders. Ah say it mus have more to Carnival dan dat.

De followin year now, ah say ah not goin to town at all, ah go stay home an watch Carnival on TV. But friends as usual, find dat is ah waste of time. Dey say, 'Well if yu go watch mas, why stay home? See it in livin colour. Come down wit us by de Savannah, is de best ting, we go sit down under ah Banyan tree, watch de mas, drink we rum, an eat plenty food. What more yu want dan dat?' Ah say OK. It wasnt ah bad idea, but de problem was de food. Dey bring Souse. Now Souse is ah funny ting. Is not any an everybody could make Souse. If yu see de Souse. Ah dont know where dey get de pig, but it was like ah pig of great experience, hard. An de souse had so much hair on it yu could ah comb it, like dey never clean de pig. Ah say dese people tryin to kill me.

Ah say it mus have more to Carnival dan dat.

Well de followin Carnival ah say ah takin it light, ah eh goin an eat no bad food again. Den me partner in Rotary tell me, 'Why yu dont come an help we in de bar? Is de best place to be. Yu could lime all day, talk-up nice woman, an yu could see all dem bands when dey passin!'

Well boy, dat was a mistake. Yu ever work in ah bar servin Trinidadians? Never in dis life again. Dem people is someting else. Ah mean yu tryin to do yu best, big band comin down de road, bout five thousan thirsty natives want someting to wet dey throat, an all ah dem want it at de same time, an yu think dey care? Care where. Ah man say, 'Ah want ah beer!' Poor you push down yu hand in de barrel to get ah beer. Yu ever put yu hand down in ah barrel ah ice-water to get ah beer? Temperature down dey bout ten below zero. Yu hand near freezin off. Ah bring up ah Carib. Cold. Hear him, 'I dont drink Carib, ah want a Stag!' Ah nearly knock him down. If he think dat I was puttin my hand back dey for he, he lie. Hear me. 'All Stag done, is only Carib it have!' Who tell you he eh drink Carib! Not me an dem. Dey callin yu all kinda ting, 'Aye you, Big Head. Watch me over here. Yu deaf or what? Yu dont serve 'left side'?' Ah want three paper cup wit ice, no make dat five. An two rum an coke, an ah red sweet drink. Dont forget de straws. Yu have change for ah hundred?' Me an bar? Ah say it must have more to Carnival dan dat.

So ah take a long rest from Carnival after dat. Den Minshall come on de scene, an me troubles start again. Quite where ah livin, quiet at home, dey come by me. If you hear dem, 'Forget dem oletime Bandleader, go an play wit Minshall, play *concept*, progressive mas.' Ah go by Minshall. Well, when yu go by Minshall an dem kinda big bands, yu dont look at de costume first, yu look at de prices — six hundred, five hundred, three hundred — when ah reach by my kinda price, about fifty dollars, ah look up to see wha dat is. Ah say dat is my section, fifty dollars.

Dat year Minshall play Zodiac. My section was call de Milky Way, was ah kinda Fancy Sailor section, all white, an Minshall put all kinda stars, an stars scatter bout de pants foot, so me two foot look like ah fire-cracker dat gone off, all me foot star-up. An on top ah dat, he design someting like ah Spiderman Mas! Yu know de kind ah net-business Spiderman does wear in de Comic Books? He design dat. De ting look nice in de drawin, but try an put it on. Is only ah man wit ah straight nose could design someting like dat.

When I put on Minshall Spiderman Mas, me nose flatten down, me lip spread back, me ears wrap around, me eyelash gone inside me eye, all me hair come down over me forehead, an people lookin at me as if ah goin an rob de Bank, like in dem movies, we all goin down de road like dat, like Bank Robbers. Well boy, we had to wrap it up, an roll it up, an put it on we head. An people only lookin at us an sayin, 'Allyu wearin stocking on allyu head!' Ah say it must have more to Carnival dan dat.

Dats when dey encourage me to become ah Stormer. De nex year dey tell me, 'Boy, listen, do like me, dont join no band, put yu money in yu pocket, put yu food dey, an go an stand up on Victoria Avenue, an lime. An every band dat pass, jump in it. So yu jump in an yu jump out, dat way yu could jump up wit every band in town for de whole Carnival, an yu eh payin no money.'

Ah say dat is my kinda mas. So ah gone on Victoria Avenue, an ah limin dey, waitin for dem band to come down. But ah make ah mistake, ah jump in de wrong band first. Ah see dis big band comin down de road, about ten thousan people in de band, an everybody in de band weighin over three hundred pounds — McWilliams comin down de road — an he playin some kinda fruits an vegetables, Breadfruit, Dasheen, Yam, Hibiscus, all kinda ting, real Agriculture comin down de road.

But I didnt know dat. I jump in de Potato Section. Ah jump between two three-hundred pound potato. Dey mash me flat. De last ting ah remember, as dey puttin me in de Ambulance on me way to hospital, was ah fella sayin, 'Is like he play in de Mash Potato Section!'

Myth, Art, Spirit (Mas) on the Caribbean Stage

RAWLE GIBBONS

In the English-speaking Caribbean, an event such as this, celebrating the region's creative talent without political pappyshowing, could happen only in Jamaica. Whatever the challenges besetting this country there is a tradition of gentility and generosity toward the arts that is part of a national ethos. I have benefited directly from this culture since my first contact with Jamaica in 1970.

The 1970s was a period of tremendous transition and revolt. This was the post-Vietnam world of political and race protests, and in the Caribbean the University of the West Indies (UWI) campuses were theatres of this wider turmoil. From Mona, students had marched into the streets of Kingston in 1968, confronting police forces against the banning of Dr Walter Rodney. In the early months of 1970, students had closed down the Creative Arts Centre on this campus, taking issue with policies regarding the use of the space by non-UWI interests. Up to the mid 1970s, in fact, the academic year routinely started with our locking down the campus for one reason or another. We burnt gowns, berated the bourgeoisie (while managing somehow to get ourselves a degree or two) but, most of all, ignited an excitement in the arts that must have been reminiscent of the Federal era.

The artists of the late 1940s to 1960s were our institution-builders. Following the pioneers of the 1930s, they would establish our Little Carib Theatre, Jamaica's National Dance Theatre Company, the Trinidad Theatre

Workshop, the West Indian novel. Drawing on the cultural richness of the region, they had defined and developed an art so characteristically and indisputably West Indian, that we, coming after, could challenge the world from positions of confidence. It is the task of every generation indeed, to push beyond the boundaries of the past. Looking back thirty-odd years, the ways in which my generation sought to do this, helps me explain, I hope, what I try to do today as a theatre practitioner.

In the first place, we saw that Africa had been suppressed or marginalized in the consciousness and tastes of the mainstream aesthetic (not, mind you, in the popular imaginary). Fuelled by the fervour of the Black Power Movement, our work focused on African consciousness as a primary and central concern. Second, we challenged the primacy placed on the written word. Inspired by the poems of Louise Bennett and Kamau Brathwaite, we admitted calypsonians, rapso artists and dub poets to the canon. Black Power formed a revolutionary creative alliance between the intended 'educated elite' and the very sources of popular art. One such forum in Trinidad was the Black Traditions series of concerts run by NJAC. In Jamaica I recall the riveting readings of Brathwaite's poems by Rastafarian Mortimer Planno, and Marina Maxwell's Yard Theatre, which inspired my own efforts in Trinidad later in the 1970s. Barbados had Yoruba Yard run by Elombe Mottley. We were also aware that though literature may be of immense value to the literate:

a)   There were other aesthetic languages used by people to express their deepest relationships within the cosmos, with others and with themselves: Haitians chose painting and iron-work, for instance; Jamaicans music and the culture of dance (hall), while Trinidadians spoke through the performing arts of Carnival.

b)   Our root impulse as Caribbean people was toward the subversion of the 'standard' language — even in its acquisition. Whether through creole or calypso, masking or mamaguyism, speechifying or the syntactical inversions of Rastafari, we delight in the subversive power that rests in the performance of the word.

c) In any case, in spite of official statistics, most school leavers were only functionally literate at best. This situation is even worse today.

Third, this validation of the oral tradition also led to experimentation with form that, I think, marked the work of our era. In Suriname, Henk Tjon brought to the stage ceremonies and rituals of the Maroon nations and the winti of Afro-Surinamese religions. In Trinidad, Victor Questel drew on Spiritual Baptist practices of trumping and doption for the rhythm and structure of his poems and plays. At Mona, we mounted Marina Maxwell's *Play Mas*, seeking to synthesize the political and aesthetic revolutions. The climax of all these efforts, however, would be Dennis Scott's seminal *An Echo in the Bone*, using possession ritual as dramatic motif and theatrical mechanism in a confrontation with history that is communally cathartic. At the heart of the experiments, to my mind, is the quest for a more inclusive and complex representation of Caribbean reality, one that not only acknowledges but is instructed by the African presence in the region and prepared to take this to its aesthetic/political conclusions.

On reflection, I would want to view the foregoing as the 'sensibility' fostered by the events of this period of history, as against suggesting generation in terms of 'age' as the defining criterion. As much as one finds a polarization of positions at such times, there is also a crunching and convergence of interests across perceived boundaries. Older artists and critics also contributed significantly to this movement of the 1970s. I refer in particular to the bold, throbbing acclamations of Africa in Rex Nettleford's classic choreographic pieces and to Gordon Rohlehr's work in broadening our perspectives on the tools and materials of literary criticism, without in any way compromising the rigour required of that discipline.

In terms of my own work, a lasting legacy of this formative period has been my choice not to make literature, as much as do theatre. This is not meant to sound pretentious and I can't say what it feels like to write fiction or poetry, for instance, at a sustained level, but writing for theatre implies in a most physical way the immediacy of an audience. The people for whom one writes are not a vague, imaginary community, but a felt and feeling presence in every breath the work takes. This immediacy drives one's responses even today, in that I find myself increasingly interested in the process, more perhaps than the product, the playing at least as much as the play. Like the rest of us, one is anxious about the relationship between one's drop-in-the-bucket efforts and the deadly social dramas playing out around us daily. The theatre process may be something of an antidote to this destruction as is our present celebration of creativity. In collective creation, all are engaged in a process of inclusion and shared ownership. I would like to think that people experiencing theatre in this way develop understandings about decision-making, reflection and responsibility that help in the building or defence of democratic institutions at the community or national level. In bringing people together as makers and sharers, theatre can become a catalyst for the creation or re-making of community.

There is another sense in which the work is about community, in that theatre is a medium for the ancestral presence — the presence of all our ancestors whose stories are not yet told in the first person. These could be First Nation, European, African, Chinese, Indian — Caribbean people. This is where history becomes spirit and spirit, being.

I wrote a play, *I, Lawah*, in 1983, dealing with the 1881 Canboulay Riots in Trinidad. That event was a defining moment in Carnival history when police attempted to confiscate the sticks and torches used by maskers in the pre-dawn Canboulay procession. The play's central character is Sophie Bella (the historical name of a stick-fighting jamette woman). She leaves the barrack yard where her child has died to work as a live-in maid with a French Creole family. When the daughter of that family immolates herself in protest against an arranged marriage, Sophie catches the power of fire which takes her from house to the street in confrontation with the police out to ban the Canboulay. The play ends with the Inspector-General who tries to arrest her spinning in possession as the fire roars on.

In writing my most recent play, *Ogun Iyan*, this woman re-appears as, for the most part, an unspeaking character. The play is based on the birth of the steelband in the late 1930s. The woman appears at 3:00 p.m. each day hovering above the boys (Kanga, Bull, Cutter, Bembeh) working on their pans down in the Dry River. We learn from them that her name is Irene Shango and that, a few years before, she suddenly stopped talking. She is considered mad and, possibly, a whore. As boys do, they make jokes about her. In the power, however, they are told that she carries a secret important to their work. They try to approach her; she evades them. When she is good and ready she descends on them in the Dry River:

(Irene approaches the camp)

KANGA: You want a seat, Miss Irene?

IRENE: I ain't sure. You all able?

CUTTER: Able with what, Miss Irene?

IRENE: Shh! If they only know where it is, they will try to thief it, to
          out it. They still vex, you know. Butler beat them. Trouble,
          trouble to find him. Look how he had them from country to
          town and when they do find him, is gone it gone. They still
          vex and they searching, so watch them, watch out for them.

CUTTER: We watching, Miss Irene.

IRENE: And if you find what you looking for, you think you able?
          You is just boys. Any of you could carry that weight like a
          woman?

BULL: I Bull, could carry anything a woman could carry.

IRENE: It ain't muscle. We does bring children. We know what it is to
          tote tomorrow, and when time burst through your bones like
          bamboo the scream it bring we know is just the beginning.
          Butler was a big man when they call him and before he, the
          Captain had class and colour on he side. Maisie Prince son,
          you able to put the weight of history round your neck and
          walk?

KANGA: History, Miss Irene?

IRENE: Before I born the Red House burn
          With the rage of the people, a rage going back they say, long
          before Canboulay.

BEMBEH: Canboulay?

IRENE: The battle for Carnival.

KANGA: I hear bout that from my grandfather. It happen right there by Hell Yard.

CUTTER: Who win?

IRENE: We here still. They feel power is in a uniform or a gun, but we does make kambule. Chupid. They feel that don't stand for nothing? That we don't count? Oh, they come to arrest him, like if we not there, like we is nothing. I stand up and say, 'No! Never!'

CUTTER: In Canboulay?

IRENE: 'Will you let them take the Chief Servant?' I was there to answer. The police over there, that Corporal King, always brutalizing black people, had him jack up like some old thief when them self was protecting the real thieves who running the oilfields. 'Will you let them arrest the Chief Servant?' he ask again and both times we shout, 'No!' Thousands of we with one voice.

BULL: Butler in Fyzabad. My mother was there too. Nearly everybody in my area who working, working in the oilfields. They say when that crowd charge, police let go bullet, who fall, fall, but nobody ain't stop. When Charlie King see the crowd serious, he let go Butler and start to run!

IRENE: Shhh! Manicou running. Look, he pelt so.

BULL: Running wild!

IRENE: He shoulda stand up and face we like a man. It woulda be quicker. Some mother mighta even see she child in he face and hold back, pause, so he coulda call on the Maker. Dog, he was, he run. *(Pause)*

KANGA: Miss Irene?

BULL: Chang Kong shop, they say, he dash in to hide. When they follow him, he try to jump through a window, but didn't know it had a drain below, fall inside there and break he foot.

IRENE: Bawling, oh, how he bawl for help, the beast turn baby, but he wasn't fooling we. We did take too much, who stone the dog, who looking to beat him with iron. I push past the Chinee, grab a tin of pitch oil and pitch that on the beast. Then I take off my petticoat, slow, wrap it in a ball, light it good and let it fly. He scream, scream, scream, til he stop. I silence Charlie King. *(Pause)* You playing with fire, Maisie son, you better have the belly of a woman.

(Rises. Exits)

Somehow in the power of her coming, Irene Shango knew she was Sophie Bella and that her story would conclude not in *Ogun Iyan* — though the steelband would be born out of fire and steel — but in the story of ashes re-igniting. A woman womb-dead or whose child shows no signs of life in the womb, gives birth. This is the first of the three plays written on Sophie, *Shepherd* (1980), which Dennis Scott helped me to understand. Her story circles back toward itself in ways I neither planned nor anticipated, a voice insistent on being heard.

I have no theory about this kind of experience, really. Perhaps she is the only kind of woman character I can write. I don't know, but, as I told myself long ago 'trust the form'. I have found, because we mask/code/ even deny so much of our genuine lives, the task of interpretation starts with listening for the embedded voice. At the same time, one is aware of the responsibility as a maker of myths for a people fragmented, to use whatever is at one's disposal — paint, sound, movement, language — to link the pieces across space, stories, time and its seas. This is what Carnival, of course, does so inimitably: invent dramas of origin, rebirth, identity, so that the fragments, worn as history, are fingered into something surprising and new.

The Calypso Theatre Experiment: Dominica 1972–1980

ALWIN BULLY

Recently in Dominica, the Department of Culture staged a festival of four of my plays from the late 1960s and the 1970s as part of DOMFESTA, a sort of local, mini CARIFESTA that was established in 1980 to celebrate Emancipation. Among them were two political dramas: *Streak!* (1975) and *The Nitebox* (1977). The former dealt with the revolt of the youth against 'the establishment' and the arrival and impact of Rastafarian philosophies on Eastern Caribbean society; the latter used the cover of a murder mystery to discuss the pros and cons of a civil service strike that had rocked the island earlier that year.

The two plays typify the work that was done by the People's Action Theatre (PAT) from 1972 when it was formed by Daniel Caudeiron and myself from what had been the Little Theatre Movement (no relation to the Jamaican model). The LTM itself had sprung from the Secondary Schools Drama Society which had been created by the four Secondary Schools of the island that had come together in 1964 to perform *The Merchant of Venice* in celebration of the 400th anniversary of the birth of William Shakespeare. I suppose that must have been as good an introduction to political drama as any, but I'm not certain that what happened in *Streak* and *The Nitebox* and the other political dramas of the period was exactly what The Bard had in mind.

In 1966 Dominica had been granted Associated Statehood with Britain, a form of semi-independence whereby the country governed its internal affairs while external affairs and defence remained the responsibility of Britain as the former Mother Country. This was intended as a training period leading to full independence and the country was full of hope and expectancy. Edward Oliver LeBlanc had brought the Dominica Labour Party to power from its grass root workers union origins, had become the island's first Chief Minister and then its first Premier. He was an astute, sensitive man who wrote poetry and had a clear vision for the betterment of his island. It seemed, however, that he was unprepared for the jostling for power and position that began in the mid 1970s among the younger, more politically ambitious members of his party as independence loomed larger.

The mandate of the PAT was unapologetically political. It embarked upon its mission in 1972 with a piece entitled *Speak Brother Speak* penned by Caudeiron and directed by myself. It ran for 15 performances — unheard of before in Dominica — and was a hit at the first CARIFESTA in Guyana the same year. The play, which extolled the virtues of the Black Power Movement and exposed the hypocrisies of society and politicians, instantly ruffled the feathers of the government. To make matters worse, Caudeiron hosted a popular Saturday morning radio programme called *Teenage Tempo* which gave voice to young disenfranchized people who had hitherto never had such an opportunity. Their views on the performance of the political directorate were far from complimentary.

At the same time the main players in the PAT began to 'publish' a literary pamphlet initially called *Free Your Mind* and later *Wahseen (Roots)* which, through poetry, short stories and reviews of popular calypso, reggae and cadance music, reflected the views expressed in the plays and by the young radicals on the radio.

Enough was enough. Caudeiron and I were summoned to a meeting with Cabinet where we were reminded that satire was one thing but that lampooning of the government was an entirely different story. In other words, we should watch it. We were sent home with a stern warning.

We were not deterred. Caudeiron actually turned up the heat on *Teenage Tempo*. The government retaliated by banning the programme and transferring Caudeiron to a desk job in one of the ministries. In 1974, angry and frustrated, he migrated to Canada where he still resides.

I was therefore left to carry the PAT torch alone, and I soon realized that I had to find a way to do so without getting burned or having the whole theatre movement go up in flames. I turned to the music traditions of the island and more specifically the contemporary popular forms of Calypso, Cadance, Cadance-lypso, Zouk and Reggae.

Dominican Protest Music

The history of Dominican protest music goes back to the Masquerade tradition of the Chante Mas or Masquerade Song. Dominica's Masquerade is as old as Trinidad's. The words 'carnival' and 'calypso' or 'kaiso' came into usage along with the arrival of the steelband from Trinidad in the 1950s. Before that, the music for the two pre-Lenten days of revelry on the streets of Roseau was the Chante Mas or the Passio which was accompanied by the Lapeau Cabwit or goat-skin drum. The lead singer, called the Chantwelle, was always a woman who would dance backwards in front of the band sending the call to the following revellers who would respond with the lavway. These songs would be dedicated to the exposure of the society's greatest ills, to derision of the upper classes and the police, and to opening up and airing local scandals (usually involving sexual relationships) and a general levelling of all and sundry.

The use of masks by all participants, particularly in Bann Mauvais and Sensay costumes (both strong African retentions still popular in Dominican Carnival today), provided anonymity and consequently greater freedom of speech. When the Chante Mas morphed into the Kaiso, and the Calypso competitions began in the early 1960s, the political satire and social commentary became even more biting. Today the social commentary is by far the more popular form of kaiso, albeit with a faster more zouk-influenced tempo than its Trinidadian counterpart.

At the same time the development of Cadance-lypso, a hybrid of Haitian Cadance and Compa music with Kaiso, created by Gordon Henderson of the Dominican band Exile One, carried the Chante Mas to another level, maintaining the use of the Kweyol language and marketing it more towards the French islands of Martinique and Guadeloupe where it was further transformed into Zouk music. At the height of the Cadance era in the mid-70s there were 18 bands producing protest music in Kweyol in Dominica — far more than the island's small population could sustain. Most of them migrated to Guadeloupe and from there to France and on to Francophone Africa. The music again explored issues of social, political and historical concern, all with an infectious syncopated driving dance rhythm which is still prevalent in the Eastern Caribbean today.

And thirdly, coming from Jamaica at the same time was reggae music led by Bob Marley, Peter Tosh, Bunny Wailer and other conscious reggae music artists of that incredible period.

My theory was therefore simple and straightforward: If these musicians could deliver messages that were politically and socially conscious, intelligent, deep, exciting, thought-provoking, stimulating, popular, understood and embraced by all levels of society, then so could the PAT and the theatre movement in general. With that, the Calypso theatre experiment began.

The Task

The task was to, first of all, transform what passed as theatre from a genteel pastime of light British comedies and Gilbert and Sullivan musicals into a serious political commentary that nonetheless entertained the public through the use of traditional art forms that resonated at all levels of society.

Early groundwork had been done in that area by Mabel Cissy Caudeiron, Daniel's mother, who can be regarded as the 'Miss Lou' of Dominica. A pioneering folklorist, in the 1950s she had brought dignity to Dominica's Creole culture, pointing out the beauty of the language, the traditional costume, the folk music and dance, the folklore, the cuisine and natural beauty.

The second part of the task was to develop an audience with improved skills in artistic criticism, an appreciation for serious drama (which does not mean dry, humourless drama), an understanding of metaphor, symbolism and allegory in storytelling, and which could look to the theatre as a source of education as well as entertainment.

The process was carefully planned and systematically delivered. Having spontaneously started with *Speak Brother Speak*, it became more structured with *Streak* in 1975. In that play I introduced performance poetry techniques which used the rhythms of the kaiso and created audience participation with the call and response convention of the masquerade revellers' Chante Mas and the calypso. Storytelling and allegory were also introduced. For example, towards the end of the play one character tells a 'conte' in the kweyol tradition of storytelling. It is clearly an allegory of the overarching theme of the entire play. The audience was quick to pick it up and make the appropriate connections. Their approval was reflected in articles and letters to the editor of the *Dominica Chronicle*, the *Herald* and the *Star* newspapers.

Streak ran for 35 performances and toured to Barbados and Saint Lucia where the response was the same.

The process had started, and Dominica and the Eastern Caribbean were rife with material and a political climate begging for public discussion and debate.

The Political Setting

It was the pre-independence era in what is now known as the Organization of Eastern Caribbean States (OECS) which currently comprises Antigua and Barbuda, Dominica, Grenada, Saint Lucia, St. Kitts and Nevis, St. Vincent and the Grenadines, and Montserrat, with Anguilla and the British Virgin Islands having observer status. Soon after independence, Dominica and Grenada experienced major social and political changes of the type that often accompanies the transition from colonial rule to self-government.

At the start of the 1970s the Black Power Movement which was thriving in the United States was taking root in the Caribbean, and talk of revolution was rife. The Black Power Revolution in Trinidad had rocked the region and the social order based on class and colour was being rapidly dismantled. In Grenada the New Jewel Movement was formed in 1973.

In Dominica the Rastafarian movement was well established by the first quarter of the decade. A group known as the Dreads took to the hills and began attacks on people perceived as 'Babylon'. Patrick John who had succeeded Edward LeBlanc as premier, and of whom more will be said, was determined to rid the island of the Dreads. This happened only after an all-out war, fought in the forests of Dominica between the Dreads and a combined unit of the Police and Defence Force in which several Dreads were killed. In the process, the government passed the highly controversial Dread Act (1974) which gave citizens the right to shoot and kill any Dread intruding on their property. The Premier of the country soon declared himself Colonel of the Defence Force and informed the House of Assembly that he had been the recipient of a Doctorate in Philosophy.

Dominica achieved independence in 1978. The following year John attempted to pass the Seditious and Undesirable Publications Act. There was massive public opposition to this, and violent protest demonstrations led to clashes with the Defence Force in which one person was shot and killed and several others injured. This resulted in a general strike which ended 18 days later, only after the entire government had resigned. Following this relatively peaceful revolution, the Committee for National Salvation, comprising a cross-section of opposition politicians and public-minded citizens, ran the country for ten months, mainly preparing for fresh general elections which ushered in the Freedom Party, with their leader, Eugenia Charles, becoming the region's first female Prime Minister. In 1979 Hurricane David, one of the fiercest of the century, devastated the island.

In 1981, Ex-Prime Minister Patrick John attempted a coup with the aid of American mercenaries, some of whom had Ku Klux Klan connections. They failed, and John was arrested, tried and imprisoned. Other ex-members of the Defence and Police Forces who had supported John in this scheme were imprisoned and one was executed.

The Grenada Revolution took place in 1979. In 1983, the United States invaded Grenada and dismantled the revolutionary government, all with the support of Eugenia Charles, as chair of the OECS, and the tacit approval of most CARICOM governments.

It was this politically charged environment that created the Dominican theatre movement of the 1970s, and became the central theme for me as Artistic Director and playwright to the People's Action Theatre.

The works that ensued and reflected all this were as follows:

PLAYS

Streak and *The Nitebox* (Bully), both already discussed; *The Ruler* (Bully), an adaptation for stage of St. Vincent's G.C.H. Thomas's political novel *Ruler in Hiroona*, loosely based on the careers of various OECS political leaders of the period; *Ti Jean Epi Few'y* and *Wev Assou Morne Makak*, kweyol translations (Bully) of Derek Walcott's *Ti Jean and His Brothers* and *Dream on Monkey Mountain*, both highly politically charged; *Folk Nativity* (Bully and LeBlanc), a Caribbean nativity musical with socio-political overtones; *Pio-Pio* (Bully), a musical on the theme of independence and self-governance; *Birth Suffer Ticket* (Bully), a performance poetry concept on the plight of the oppressed; *Pele* (Bully), an exposé of the political intrigues that trapped thirty-two thousand people in the volcanic eruption of 1902 (performed in workshop only); *Jeanne d'Arc Meets Copain Lapin* (Bully), an examination of relationships between Guadeloupeans and Dominicans in the aftermath of Hurricane David; *Jesus Christ Superstar* (Webber and Rice), the musical on the Passion of the Christ emphasizing the political influences therein; *The Sea at Dauphin* (Walcott), *Shango de Ima* (Cuba) *Diablotin* (Dixon), *The Rose Slip* (Archibald), *Moon on a Rainbow Shawl* (John), *How Johnny Break de Spell* (Caudeiron), *Belle Fanto* (Roach), adapted into a musical (Bully); *McB*, an adaptation of Shakespeare's Scottish play (Bully), in which Mr and Mrs McBee switch roles in the middle of the story. (This play was written and performed in 1988 but is included here in view of its intense political theme strongly reflecting the Jamaican and Caribbean landscape at the end of the 1980s and its connection with the earlier series.)

RADIO SERIALS

Green Gold (Bully), a radio soap opera, teaching best banana growing practices; *Secrets of La Cloche* (Bully), best practices in public health; *Winds of Change* (Bully), survival post hurricane, recovery and rehabilitation; *Fire Go Burn* (Bully and O'Marde), family planning best practices.

The Political Drama

It is said that all writing is political, but all writing does not set out to be political. From the onset the People's Action Theatre carried a strong, if not blatant, political agenda. It recognized the power of theatre in effecting social change and critical thinking and carefully selected work which gradually radicalized its public, becoming increasingly sophisticated in its methodologies with each performance. The times in which the PAT operated called for such thinking as a support mechanism in the birth of a nation. The independence period in these islands was fraught with misgivings about change and the injustices of colonialism versus the potential abuse of power in the creation and interpretation of the new constitutions. The Trade Union Movement, which had benefited the working class and was human rights oriented through and through, had already had its internal leadership battles, and the public feared that these would grow worse once independence had been gained. In Dominica these fears were immediately justified with the antics of Patrick John who was clearly heading in the direction of many Latin American and African dictators who had declared themselves President for Life soon after being elected to office. The suppression of freedom of speech, including freedom of the press, was evident within a year of John's tenure, and his attempted coup in 1983 was further evidence of his desperate bid for complete control of the island. The events in neighbouring Grenada followed a similar pattern.

While there has been no scientific evaluation of the impact of the People's Action Theatre on political thought in Dominica in the 1970s, the vibrant response of audiences to the ideas expressed on stage cannot be doubted. Following each production, the many letters that appeared in

The *Dominica Chronicle* and other newspapers reflect a level of political consciousness based on themes carried by the plays, often linking them to the actual situation that they portrayed or parodied. It was widely rumoured at one stage that plans were afoot to have the theatre company censored and scripts vetted by government with the intention of curtailing productions with heavy political overtones. This action was never taken, however; probably because it would most likely only have increased the popularity of the productions, as had been the case with calypsos given this treatment in the past.

The need to be careful was also brought home to the company when Yvonne Brewster saw *The Ruler* while scouting the region for suitable theatre productions to be staged as part of CARIFESTA II in Jamaica in 1976. While she thought that the piece was one of the finest she had seen in the Eastern Caribbean, she warned us that showing it in Jamaica might have serious political repercussions as it so closely reflected the history of Jamaican politics and the actions of their leaders and supporters. As a result the play was not taken to the festival.

In Dominica, the threats to the existence of political theatre were never from party supporters but only from the government of the day, who clearly felt threatened by such frank criticism. As artistic director of the company I was never personally attacked or victimized. As a teacher at the government-owned Dominica Grammar School (the oldest educational institution in the island and one of the largest) my work was highly appreciated and at age 27 I was appointed acting headmaster. When I informed the minister of education that I planned to leave teaching and the civil service to pursue a career as a playwright and director, he offered me a job as Dominica's first Director of Culture, whose task it was, naturally, to create a Department of Culture. I accepted the position and that post, along with married life and starting a family, brought my writing career to a virtual standstill. While the People's Action Theatre continued to function under the direction of the assistant artistic director, Nigel Francis, its performances became less frequent and in the 1980s no original works were staged. The company's role as political commentator by all intents and purposes was over. I moved to Jamaica in 1987 to take up a UNESCO post and most other members of the company migrated also — mainly to the United States where some of them have pursued theatre careers. Those who remained in Dominica continue to perform occasionally, so that the company cannot be said to be extinct.

Looking back on the work of the People's Action Theatre and various other 'conscious' theatre groups in the 1970s with their clear commitment to political and social transformation, theatrical offerings in the Caribbean today are surprisingly tame. The arts of the 1970s reflected the sense of excitement and adventure that accompanied the coming of independence. People of the region were filled with hope and self confidence; they felt that they were finally in control of their own destiny and the world was their oyster. It was a time to celebrate themselves, their history, heritage and culture; it was also a time for the artist to join the politicians in mapping the way forward, giving direction, putting up warning signs, guarding against pitfalls, reminding politicians and populace to remain well grounded even while their spirits soared. This artistic leadership was exemplified in Jamaica in Marley's music, the work of the National Dance Theatre Company, the Sistren Theatre Collective, the Jamaica School of Drama, the film *The Harder They Come*, the art of Edna Manley, the writing of John Hearne and Orlando Patterson, the poetry of Miss Lou, to name a few; in Trinidad by the rise of pan music, the calypso giants like The Mighty Sparrow and Lord Kitchener, the carnival arts, the dance of Beryl McBurnie, the art of Leroy Clarke, the literature of Naipaul, Derek Walcott and the Trinidad Theatre Workshop; in Guyana it was the genius of Mittelholzer, the paintings of Aubrey Williams and Philip Moore; in Barbados the little magazine *Bim* which brought writers from around the region to the fore, the Barbados Writers Workshop; in St. Lucia the Arts Guild, the work of the Walcott brothers Derek and Roderick, the poetry of Robert Lee, the art of Dunstan St. Omer; in St. Vincent and the Grenadines the work of Cecile 'Blazer' Williams and the New Artists Movement; in Antigua, that of Dorbrene O'Marde and his Harambee Theatre; in Dominica cadance-lypso and calypso music, the Swinging Stars Dance Band, the National

Day folk festival and the People's Action Theatre; and the list could go on and on — in each island the artist giving direction, exhorting the people to think while they celebrate.

The euphoria did not last long. In the case of Dominica and Grenada, in particular, the new freedom soon turned sour and the dreams came crashing down, as political greed, in-fighting and power struggles took precedence over nation building and economic growth. It was at that point that conscious theatre groups came into their own.

These groups were fortunate in that they enjoyed a large degree of freedom of speech. I am not aware of censorship of plays being practised in any Anglophone Caribbean country at that time. The political writers of the day were therefore under no pressure to curtail their ideas or go underground. It might be due to this very liberty that there are so few political playwrights in the region today — the open arena offered no challenge, no adrenaline rush.

In those years I saw myself as a political writer with a mission to use theatre as a tool for political and social transformation. I see this as the duty of the artist. I think most conscious musicians see themselves the same way. All tools at our disposal should be pressed into service for national and regional development.

Tenky Miss Lou, Tenky

JOAN ANDREA HUTCHINSON

Mi is a bawn Jamaican an mi proud proud proud
An yuh fi feel proud too
Fi walk roun an big up yuh ches
An say tanks to Miss Lou

Wen she did start she never know
A how it woulda go
An nuff nuff people wen dah laugh
An call her pappy show

But she galang strong an stick it out
For she know say she did right
Inna her belly battam she did know one day
Dem woulda see di light

Entime trouble teck wi a Miss Lou wen
Put wi good name pon di map
An wen dah push Jamaica heritage
An lawd, she wouldn stop

She say 'Teck kin teet kibba heart bun'
Wen times never so sweet
'Good luck will come as long as fowl
Dah scratch up dungle heap'

Nuff a dem wen tink say she crazy
An nuff meck up dem face
How Miss Lou a chat dis boogooyagga patwa
All over di place

For dem wen tink patwa was bad English
Dem never know poor ting
Dem wouldn tell dem pickney Nancy story,
An folk song dem wouldn sing

But a di jackass wid him long tail
Bag a cocoa comin dung
An di peel head johncrow pan tree top
Jus meck dem head spin rung

An lickle bi lickle dem start fi back her
Start fi fan her flame
An see deh after fifty year
Miss Lou a one household name

Now wi nuh shame fi chat wi owna language
An wi dah tank yuh fi it Miss Lou
Dem a teach it clear up a university
An ongle sake a you

Dem a meck flim, an dem a write book
Dem a sing whole heap a song
An a say 'Oh patwa is a good language'
But yuh wen know dat all along

So now wi tan up proud fi be Jamaican
An wi waan di world fi hear
Miss Lou nuff tanks, for howdy and tenky
Never bruck nuh square

Ivan Lef Mi Inna Grief

If yuh did tell mi say people could a so wicked
Mi would a tell yu say 'A lie'
But todda day hurricane Ivan pass through Jamaica
And lef mi poor gyal a cry

Mi nay a halla becaw storm blow way mi house
And lef mi inna grief
Never bawl causen say mi ackee tree blow dung
But becaw people too tief

Tief! Mi say croomoogin an red yie
Badmine an jus tan bad
Tief! becaw dem kin ever a cratch dem
Fi weh adda people have

Tief! becaw dem nuh know how fi satisfy
Jus like di dawg an di bone
Tief! becaw dem nuh know how fi cut dem yie
An lef people tings alone

Di radio announce say big breeze blow a come
An fi mi granny she jump up
She say 'Gyal, Courts have plenty nice tings up deh
Gwaan go try yuh luck'

She say before Gilbert fi her house did empty so till
She couldn't even smile
But him gi her fridge, TV an microwave
Meck she a live inna style

So mi pack cawfee, crackers an two tin a mackerel
An of course mi pack mi chimmy
Fi go camp out front a Courts whole night fi see
Weh Ivan a go gi mi

Mi waan one new fridge an one microwave
Entertainment centre an big screem TV
One divan, an aldoah mi nuh know a wah
Mi waan one DVD

But di Courts people put up one rhatid storm shutter
Not even Ivan could a tear it dung
Dem nuh have nuh conscience, have mi a drench whole night
Lickle most mi drown

Wen di breeze a blow, mi haffi heng on pon one light post
An cotch pon one macca limb
Water splish splash mi an wash mi clear a woi ee woi
A good ting mi could a swim

De wet mi wet, mi a coofoom coofoom an have yeahgo
An one piece a short breath
Imagine mi bleach whole night, Ivan come an gawn
An all me get was wet

But what a hurricane wicked an purpose doah eeh
Mi nuh know a wah do Ivan
Have mi up a batter whole night, till mi sick
An lef mi wid mi two long han

Nuh bus never a run, so mi haffi walk go a Portmore
Mi cuss Ivan di whole way
Wen mi ketch a mi road, mi yie dem opin wide
Suppose yuh see how di place stay

All kine a tree trunk car part an people roof
Kyatta kyatta, di place look bad
Wen mi look, mi roof an one side a mi house gawn
Trus mi, mi nearly mad

An wen mi teck a stock, di whole a mi furnitures dem
Gawn like Sammy mout
Di croomoogin, tiefing people go inna mi house
An teck out weh dem fi teck out

If yuh did tell mi say people could a wicked so
Mi would a say 'A lie'
Fo mi never know say tief bruck house inna rain
Dat a wuss dan dry yie

So see mi yah, mi ban mi belly an mi bawl
For Ivan lef mi inna grief
Mi heart full, from mi bawn mi never know say
People kyan so tief

After Ivan:
Reflections Under the Mountain

MERLE COLLINS

The devastation caused to Grenada by Hurricane Ivan was unimaginable. I know that others who have seen the result of hurricanes in various places would want to echo the sentiments for their own experience. I can only talk about mine and Grenada. When I stood up in Marquis and watched how Ivan had picked up a boat from the beach and pulled it clear across the road to settle on the other side, I thought of revolution; I thought of murder and mayhem; I thought of invasion. When I returned to Grenada after Hurricane Ivan, I stood under the mountain that sheltered my family house and looked up. I felt relieved that I had been spared the experience by my absence, but I was also curiously uneasy because I had been away. Once again I considered the contradiction of being so often far away from all that motivates me, not just to write, but to wonder.

My family house is in a place called Morne Delice, under the Mt Gozo mountain. What I saw, in the days after Ivan, was that Mt Gozo had been totally stripped of its leaves, and the tall trees behind the house had either fallen crossways in the land or were standing tall, dry and leafless, impossibly bare. There was a twist of brown arms and *kabosé* torsos to the top of the hill. My neighbours told me that when they went up after the storm to check on the house it was completely plastered with leaves. The wind had struggled with the trees, ripped their clothes off and flung them in the face of the house that the trees protected. By the time I got there, my neighbours had painstakingly removed the leaves from the face of the house. They kept saying to me, 'This is not how it was; was not so it was, you know.' They, and others, were trying to make me see the wonder of the thing, the face of the house covered with leaves flung there by Ivan in his rage, the mountain coming to Mohamet. Ivan made me remember my father, made me anxious to write about him, how he had planted copious numbers of trees behind the house, tall trees to shade the cocoa, trees to be part of a windbreak in the land. I remembered how he exasperated us, my father, the way he talked as if he had special knowledge of the land and the wind, the way he spent so much time with his construction of 'windbreaks' and planting shade for the cocoa. We muttered about the big old heavy trees all over the land. He was a land man; we, the others in the house, were more interested in the sea, in the beach anyway, and in the life of the town close to the sea. He ignored us, didn't seem to hear us, and continued to construct his windbreaks. To be fair to us, those of us who were pulled to the town and the sea, he never tried to take us with him into the land, to help us develop that understanding of the land. What was understood was that we, the children, were meant for books and to be pushed toward the town, not to be taken inland to fathom that story. And as I watched how the naked trees held up their hands to the skies, I thought how that, too, that pushing the youth toward the sea, showed itself in party politics in September and October 1983, when the youthful revolutionary party, well-meaning but misguided, could not in the end hear the heartbeat of the land. It was only after I was grown, and had started to be able to have a discussion with my father, after the books somehow made me want to make tentative trips into the land, that I learned about trees to shade cocoa, about how sometimes the cocoa tries to reach up, as if it wants to outgrow the shade trees, about how trees sometimes reach up, struggling for each other's light, about how mortelle is the best tree to plant on a boundary line. As he told me about the struggle of the trees, he said, 'They just like people, you know.' He also showed me, there in the land, the grave of an old overseer, white, I assumed, lying forgotten in the land, among people who had no interest in him. I wondered who his descendants were and if they had any idea where his grave was.

After Ivan, as I thought of how people kept telling me they 'saw the wind', that they heard it, not sing, but howl, as they held their fingers up and swirled the index around to show me what the wind looked like as it burrowed its way toward a house, I thought of my father, of his years of building structures to be prepared for the wind. I watched the trees that took the battering as they saved the house from the wind (because nothing happened to it except that Ivan slapped it and left its imprint on the face), and realized that although I knew windbreak's name because it was so often mentioned in my house, I didn't know how it served its function. I realized that, ten years after my father's death, Ivan was leading me to a deeper appreciation of his life and I wanted to understand the things he sometimes talked about. I acknowledged, all over again, that in Grenada lie the roots to an understanding of myself and of my story, that writing for me would always be wrapped up in an understanding not only of the sea and the continuing need to wander, of the leaves, of the trees, of the mountains, of the forgotten graves.

After Ivan, when I turned away from watching the Mt Gozo mountain and looked the other way, over to Morne Jaloux and St. Paul's and down to Westerhall and then further away to Grand Anse and to the sea beyond, I could see how much clearer the place was, how Ivan had chopped off the heads of trees and stripped trees of leaves so completely that people were much nearer to each other. I realized that I could sit in Morne Delice and watch a car go around the corner in Westerhall. Over and over again, in those days after Ivan, I heard people express surprise that they could see such and such a house, that way down inside La Borie you weren't that far from the St Paul's police station or the St Paul's main road, that it was really true what people said, that the island small and no one lives very far away.

The mountain behind the house usually hides not only the house, but also the cocoa and nutmegs, the vines and all the creatures of the land — the land rats, the snakes, the manicou. Now vines were no longer climbing or clinging. I thought not only about the windbreaks I would have to find out more about, the windbreaks an entire generation of supposedly learned people my age and younger knew little about, but also about the hurricanes, natural and human, that had gone before, and, inevitably of the ones, natural and human, to come. I thought about Kick-Em-Jinny, the volcano under the sea near the island of Carriacou, about how we laughed fearfully when boats were tossed up and about over Kick-Em-Jinny; I wondered about how and why, some years ago, a number of dead fish appeared in the sea around Grenada, so that people were advised not to eat fish but advised of little else to do with the incident; I thought of how I had accidentally come across an article informing me that when Mt Pelée in Martinique erupted, years ago, the same thing had happened — dead fish had appeared in the sea around St George's. Ivan makes me wonder how much we do not know about ourselves. I cannot escape the feeling that somehow the elements write the stories before we do, and perhaps the entire history and political story of the island — of our islands — is represented in the sudden violence of Ivan, in the destructive rage of Janet in 1955, in the deceptive calm that has come again to settle over the land.

Ivan came like revolution, March 13, 1979, like murder and mayhem, October 19, 1983. When you watching the naked mountain, you remember how invasion leave you with your mouth open, feeling that the impossible happen. You looking up into that one-time garden of Eden and you remembering how they say that after the Fall, the Lord tell Adam to cover his nakedness. And is a wonder to look around and see how the nakedness getting covered in various ways. A lot of people suffer; afterwards, some people even prosper, but depending on the lesson you learn, the prosperity tenuous.

The land settling down again. The mountain dress itself, so you can't see the nakedness. But you watching it with a kind of disquiet because you tasted the fruit of destruction and already you see more than (perhaps) you should. The trees have leaves now, houses are getting hidden and people are beginning to forget again who lives on one side and on the other. But every time the wind blows and trees rustle, you jump and look over your shoulder, because you have this sense that — something in the mortar besides the pestle.

Born Inside the Stories

JEAN D'COSTA

Let me begin by explaining that I do not consider myself to be a writer. Rather, I am a person who has written down some of the thoughts that have come — in various shapes, at various times — to my mind. Some of this writing has ended up in printed form. That printed writing has been assigned to various genres. None of that matters. The thinking alone matters, for there begins everything. Long before the printed or the written page comes the thinking. There is no good term for the process of ideation that has flowed from so long ago, before I learned any language at all, and which will flow until ended by nature in due course. In its flowing, it has no real need of language: language is a final stage of shaping, a narrowing down into a communicable mode, and is itself a form of play and of music. It helps us to share thought and ideation, but it limits and it colours, and although it will at times expand into new angles of perception, it is forever tinier than thought. Language is a mode of travel, while thought fills the universe, defying time and place. Poets know this truth better, perhaps, than anyone else, but all of us know it to be true, for we are all makers of thought as well as audience to each other's expressive communications.

Some may say, 'But without language there can be no thought.' To them I reply, 'Umm-hm?' and 'Eeh-hi?' I leave the audience to determine what meanings — and how many — may be derived from that reply. And what language was used. Better yet, I utter no spoken reply: silence.

Nevertheless you, reader or hearer of this paper — *'hypocrite lecteur, mon semblable, mon frère'* — know that silence in any context is also meaningful. Beneath the silence lie your thoughts — and mine.

Let me also explain that thinking controls my mind and work. If there has been a force that compels me — and it appears that some such force does exist — it is one that intermingles discovery; play; suddenly finding the new in the familiar; the new turning out to be old, or the old, new; and a sense of sharp purpose. This last aspect is linked to the who, when and where of my history. That purpose has been to discover the nature of my place and time, and of what lies within it, and around. Such discovery has been, simply, my single most important task. That purpose is as old as I am, and its beginnings are as bright and sharp today as they were in the first four years of my life. The purpose arises from the beginning of ideation, of sentience, of awareness of place, time, and self — in that order. It arose in my first years of life, the brightest purposive moment coming in the very first year of all, 1937.

The chronology of those first years is simple and important. I was born on January 13, 1937, in my grandmother's cottage, on the edge of Kingston. My mother and I stayed there until April when we joined my father, sister, and brother at Vaughansfield, St. James. This is a rural area far inland from Montego Bay, on the edge of the Cockpit Country — Maroon country. In 1937, it was behind God's back. My parents taught at the elementary school, and had been living in the Anglican rectory, an old house on the crest of the hills above the school. We stayed in that old rectory until the end of 1937, moving to another somewhat smaller (but safer) house lower down the hillside. This was Mr Sinclair's house, and we lived there until December, 1940, when we left for Somerton, St. James, where my father took up the headship of Somerton Government School. We stayed in Somerton until December, 1944, moving to Kingston as World War II went into its final convulsions. I was by then almost eight and, in my view, fully grown up. In some ways, I suppose I must have been correct. Nothing I learned later was as hard as what I learned in those eight years, or so I told my father: language, manners, faces, gestures, the flames of many lives, arithmetic, reading, spelling, writing, yet more manners, illnesses, games, names, deaths, war, songs, fear, beliefs, reasons for beliefs, and beliefs without reason. And all of these to be committed to memory, for use at any time. These were also the official memories, approved and privileged. They were the hardest, not the most valuable. They stand apart in a separate, almost public category: the field in which I should toil, drawing on the private wellspring of memory as guide.

For many years I assumed that the personal memories I have of learning to walk, of seeing the world from below knee-height in adults, were usual and ordinary. Surely, everyone remembers not being able to reach the door knob or the wash basin, of seeing the floor miles below from the seat of a chair? When I told my parents of specific memories from the first three and four years of my life, they were able to date those memories and to place several of them in my first twelve months. The richest memories belong to the old rectory and to Mr Sinclair's house, to the first four years.

In this stream of consciousness, starting from so very early, lies my sense of self and of purpose.

In those first four years (January, 1937, to December, 1940), Jamaica was taking me and shaping me into her being. Each house we lived in during those early years stands out clearly in my memory. The old rectory is the house where I first saw, smelled, heard and explored the world of sentience, of ideation. My task and memories begin in this place. The gold September light of my first September; the dark yet faded wooden floors; the verandah steps which I descended on my behind; the thin, springy, night-scented jasmine bush growing to the left side of the front steps; the chairs whose seats lay at eye level and helped me stand, and see: all of these shapes, textures, happenings, movements and states of being told me firmly that here I had come into existence, here I should learn, here I should try to perceive, to listen, to discover, to remember, to take note even if I could not understand.

The first and earliest memory remains bathed in golden afternoon light. It was the first time I can recall seeing sunlight hang like honey, caressing the faded cream walls of the room, reflected off the furniture and floor. I was about nine months old.

I am sitting on the floor, a dark wood floor with a hint of dull red dye in it. It has small, tight, deep-dyed planks, cool and smooth, no splinters, not much shine, and I am sitting up by myself, alone, and pleased to be alone. I know I can't move by my own self. I am unworried. Sitting on the cool warm floor, clad only in a diaper, legs stretched out, balanced, I am perfectly content. Light fills the room around me, plays on the wall. Stillness fills the world.

Then comes a strange marvel. An exquisite sense of something happening inside me takes on its own being — small, then larger, a rising and blending of sensory, almost mystical signals from within. The signals become impulse, and impulse becomes action, but not of my choosing. It all just *happens.*

Then comes the true magic. A something is flowing from me, it turns into a pool of crystal clear liquid whose bright edges appear beside me. The pool grows. It is the same temperature as me. I realize that I made it, but I don't know how. All I know is that this production of mine is absolutely brilliant, something in which to rejoice.

The crystal pool widens, flowing along the floor to the skirting board, dark brown against pale cream paint. The paint is flaky. The skirting board is several shades of browny-red. Suddenly, in the midst of feeling this ambient light, and the warm upfloating air – air both warm and cool, calm and sharp, I know how alive I am.

So I decide to celebrate this new state of mine, this creation of crystalline beauty.

Up go my arms above my head, and down: SPLASH! Up again, SPLASH!

Up again — but suddenly there come explosions of horrid noise above!

Far, far above, so high up I can't see, as high as God, or Heaven, or all of those things we can't really see — from high up there come huge disapproving noises. The noises thunder down on my head and I know I have done Wrong.

Worst of all, the light of the room turns to blazing visible heat above, out of which appears a huge pair of hands, hands as big as bulldozer buckets, hands bigger than me: these great bodiless hands descend and take me up. And cut off the moment and the day. The memory ends. And there is no face to remember, only a huge voice, huge hands.

From then I knew that I saw a unique world, one which only I can truly see. Much later, I discovered that this truth belongs to every child born into this life: with each new birth comes a unique vision, a unique process of ideation and sentience. Each of you reading these words knows it to be true. You have experienced this reality even as culture beats it down and tries to make us into generalities: consider the notion that each newborn consciousness creates a single and singular view of the universe — a complete religion and purpose-of-being, a new mythos.

With this awakening into sentience and ideation came my purpose: to understand.

This task came to me from before I could use language, but not before I could perceive, think, and begin to discover the layers of behaviour that we call culture. In the voices and actions around were tones that rejoiced, warned, protested, lied, boasted, quarrelled, rebuked, chided, begged, invited, teased, played, soothed, discussed, comforted, alarmed, and argued. The voices and faces and bodies gave out showers of meaning, but much of the meaning — especially the surface meanings — escaped me then. It was the underlying cut and thrust, the drama between all the elements of this universe that held me with immense power.

I have never been released.

Without realizing what was going on, I was being conditioned as a member of an audience that is also itself the maker and singer. This double role did not show itself to my conscious mind until years later, when I discovered that the notion of 'author' is modern, and in a sense, quite thin and artificial. In the millenia of our existence, the making and sharing of thought and story have been everybody's business. It would seem as if, since the advent of printing, the Writer stands apart from the Audience, the one performing Responsibly, the other listening Respectfully. That notion is, quite simply, untrue. Some may sing better than the rest and may become habitual, sought-after singers, or we may find that some have better memories and so become custodians of experience and knowledge. We all are, however, both audience and performer, speaker and listener, thinker and explorer.

Jamaica shaped me as audience and simultaneously as observer, reporter, storyteller, historian, explainer, and entertainer. All of these elements constitute my basic being. Most important of all, I slowly learned the difference between literal, historic fact and the transcendent truth which only the storyteller and the story bring to life. Without the factuality of history, the all-important details of experience, one cannot begin to search for truth. Without the mythic vision that penetrates and brings to life the essence of experience, we cannot find the many truths that lie inside experience. Our discoveries would have no meaning or life. Without sharing in the re-visitings of essential truth, both audience and teller would starve to death.

To illustrate, my latest children's story, *Jenny and the General*,[1] just out this year from Carlong Publishers, came upon me during a very boring, very hot afternoon in a faculty meeting here at Mona. In order to entertain myself during the agony of the meeting, I scribbled the story down on the back of the minutes. In the undertow of my mind, at the time, ran the story of Sam Sharpe, Daddy Sharpe, of whom I had first heard in Vaughansfield. This talk surrounded me after we moved to the second house, when I had learned to walk and could be taken for walks. From various people on the road, around the house, came the stories, stories as real and solid as those who told them.

There in Vaughansfield, the river runs underground, They said, and runaways and rebels could walk underground from parish to parish. In the slavery days, They said, you could take the dark ways hidden behind the falls over the blue hole (it terrified me, that blue hole), and meet with Daddy Sharpe, They said. He was a kind man, a very kind man. They told me of his kindness, his care for others. They must have said much more, but it was the kindness, the protectiveness of this man who was glad to risk, and then give his life, for our sake, that held me.

I do not know why Sam Sharpe was so vivid in my mind in the mid 1970s: it may have been the effect of work on Jamaican history then current. I cannot tell. Yet, there came to my mind a child in danger, a child who is loved by one who will not yield until she is safe. I cannot explain why the story took its shape. I can say only that that afternoon, something of the pain, grandeur, and tragedy of that man took over my mind and demanded expression and assuagement. As I sit and recall the moments in which the scribbling went on, an echo of the pain and grief and triumph that underlie the making of this story re-surfaces in my mind, and once more I feel the dagger of light and sacrifice that forced the story out of me. It hurt then, it hurts now. It was worth it then, and is still worth it today.

While I was busy scribbling, I did not realize that the story had been implanted decades earlier, that its motive forces were rooted within me, gifts from the storytellers along the roads of Vaughansfield. It is only now, so many years later still, that the origins of the myth underlying this story have become clear to me. Because of the vast gift made over to me in those early years, my turn came to make a gift to the audience in which I belong. It was my turn to let the mythic power of the story live anew, in a new shape, with new agents and a new plot.

Some further explanation is due to those who will look at this children's story, and ask why should the hero be a *dog*? What possible connection could there be between a dog and this National Hero? The answer lies in character and in the kinship with other forms of life that was also shaped in me during those years in rural St. James. When my mother was alone with three small children, expecting to hear at any moment of her husband's death in hospital, it was a large, cheerful dog who lay across the front door by day and by night, and kept us safe. It was he who took three small children for walks, and if we were approached by anyone he deemed unsafe, he stood between us and the potential threat, hackles raised. He always brought us safely home. That single statement sums up the force of *Jenny and the General.*

It was also in those early years that I found out about death: her name does not return to my mind, only her tranquil, dark face. She still looks quiet and thoughtful in her cedar coffin in the Presbyterian church at Somerton, in 1941. We were newcomers there, we did not know her, but out of respect we went (along with everyone else in Somerton) to honour her and bury her. I wondered at the time what she might be thinking. I have wondered since. She had many stories to tell, I knew. Such stories, or histories, are my concern.

My parents had no idea that I had joined with the crowd of mourners and gone to see the lady in the coffin. Once they found out where I was, my mother took me off to the back of the church, somewhat worried, but I had already completed the task of meeting the lady, with the promise of not forgetting her. She gave me no sense of fear, or dread, or horror: she simply asked me to see and remember, and then try to understand. I am still trying. It is she who made me conceive 'Funeral for an Elementary School Teacher', a poem written about seven years ago. She is quite different from the teacher in the poem, but it is this lady's will to be recognized and remembered that made the poem happen.

She has presented herself to my mind in many guises, with branching stories rising up from that central moment. Her life was interwoven with the people who went on the one bus to Montego Bay, twice a week. The young men who drilled on Faulkner's Common with long poles, getting ready in case the Germans invaded, all knew her. Some may have been cousins, nephews, neighbours. Some of them went off to fight in Europe, or work in the merchant marine. The men who drank rum in the shop at Cross Roads knew her, and every man there had his share of stories, some very well known, some very well concealed. She must have known the two tiny, aged sisters in the small stone house at the top of a narrow track, two of the smallest, whitest people ever seen on earth, the Misses Colquhoun. It was fun learning and remembering how to spell their cooing Scottish name. Then there was the doctor who came from Adelphi on his horse, in the event of dire illness. In the darkness when the stars rose white over the nightscape, the stories spread and grew all over the hills and valleys.

Everything was story: beginnings, middles, and endings lay around, and from every ending came a beginning.

Paths fascinated me. A tiny track going off up a hillside meant a way into another world, another branching set of stories.

And there was the pond which I never saw, up in the hills somewhere, the pond in which some of Somerton's inhabitants had disappeared forever, They said. Those involved in making them disappear knew nothing, of course, and joined in telling stories of how dem see de bway an im fada outa Bay, a tek train fe Kingston. Perhaps there was no such pond. Perhaps there were no such disappearances. But the stories persisted.

Because these stories had such power, they fitted seamlessly into the stories read from the printed page, just as they fitted into my father's reciting of 'The Lady of the Lake', all umpteen thousand melodramatic lines of it, to distract me when I was ill with toothache and a high fever. It took him three hours to perform the poem (from memory), and at the end I came slowly back into the present world, but with no fever, no toothache. He was also given to cryptic utterances which made sense only decades later. 'We from Glengoffe in St Catherine,' he said one day to me, 'we are of the Ashanti.' He did not explain; I did not know what to ask, but he was very earnest. I was being bidden to remember: 'We are of the Ashanti.' He also told us children about the only known ancestor of the family, the Irishman John Crary, who owned land, cattle and Africans at Glengoffe. 'He died without a will, so all the people stayed on the land and took his name. That was the custom, but many of the children were actually his. After John Crary died, no one ever came to claim the property. We Crearys stayed there until Emancipation, and then some left and settled in St Mary, or went to Kingston.' At the time (I was about seven or eight), I thought my father was making up all of this. Instead of asking him sensible questions, I humoured him by agreeing to remember, never to forget, even if these stories made no sense. He gave me a branch to grasp, letting me know that its connections are alive and endless.

It has never been my desire to be a professional writer, but it has long been my desire to set down thoughts that would give enjoyment and stimulation to others. Just as conversing with strangers or friends makes one much more alive, so does the constant conversation that goes on in my mind between images, ideas, pieces of opinion, snatches of words, shapes, colours, smells, sounds. Rapid and fragmentary, these inner conversationalists will at times slow down enough for me to take dictation from them. They let me look at them and turn them around, play with them, arrange them, until suddenly they re-arrange themselves, often disappearing for good. Sometimes they force me to write them down. At times, writing them down has made me ill, for they can have terrible power and they may transport one to places where one would rather not be. At other times, they make me laugh and dance with them; they can make me cry, and they can suddenly retreat and refuse to show themselves. They can also say, 'We do not wish to be formed into words, nor do we wish to be thought out in words or written down. Words are our enemies. Language is not a friend, just a road, and we are off the road vehicles: beware!' And then some of them sidle in, looking mischievous, and come as words in seductive form, such that one cannot forget them. Then, I have to write.

I doubt whether Wilson Harris knew what he was doing — consciously — when he wrote the following lines from *Palace of the Peacock.* It is the Seventh Day, creation is complete, life and death have interflowed, and the moment of revelation rises to a musical climax branded on the reader's memory by its final line:

> The enormous starry dress [that the Tree] now wore spread itself all around into a full majestic gown from which emerged the intimate column of a musing neck, face, and hands, and twinkling feet. The stars became peacocks' eyes, and the great tree of flesh and blood swelled into another stream that sparkled with divine feathers *where the neck and the hands and the feet had been nailed.*

> This was the palace of the universe and the windows of the soul looked out and in.[2]

The line in italics is made up of four anapaests, with the strong beat falling on 'neck', 'hands', 'feet', and 'nailed', but it is the drumbeat of the two weak beats followed by the strong monosyllable ('where the neck'), and repeated three more times, that gives the paragraph its terrible, final beauty, preparing one for the next, climactic sentence. Words such as these surge from depths that cannot be controlled. Harris's genius serves to remind us that these depths exist in all of us, even if we do not find the means, as he did, of bringing out that inner world. Afterwards, sometimes, the maker or writer looks at the work and recognizes what it has been doing. Sometimes, the maker or writer can willingly set up, change, arrange the words into better patterns, but the underlying forces exist beyond our control.

They greatly resist external organization and will not allow anything to be imposed upon them as a generic or general rule. Therefore, they dictate how and what should be said (or written). They choose their diction, their place in the continuum of Jamaican language behaviour and usage — and it is one that is inbred in me. These thoughts may, for fun, allow themselves to move into forms of language in which they do not normally present themselves, but they know this game and enter it in all the energy of any good Jamaican talk. Topic, interlocutor, mood and purpose decide what forms of language we will use at any given moment.

Jamaican language is multi-form and multi-focused: its behavioural ranges are vast. During the seventeenth, eighteenth, and nineteenth centuries, Jamaica was a multilingual society. The memory of those times persists below the conscious level. In my time, linguistic performance as a social skill was shown off at weddings, at concerts, and in bars and corner shops, and the eager acceptance of polylingualism came out in phrases greedily snatched from Spanish, Norwegian, Chinese, or Hindi. In the days before my times, linguistic skill might make the difference between survival and living hell, between belonging and exclusion. Hence the many language forms that evolved between 1655 and 1807. In that Jamaica, it was normal and right that people spoke different language forms in various places, and for various reasons. On the sugar estates in the west, Chinese and Indians were among the last comers, and although their languages may appear to have died, the habit of polylingualism has not left the Jamaican subconscious.

Hence Jamaicanness demands that one use appropriate language forms for places, persons, and subject matter. At the same time, Jamaican language behaviour assigns a social context and rank to any language form within its ken. The Chinese shopkeeper should speak Chinese to her family, but she must speak to me in Jamaican creole. She may teach me some Chinese, in which case we become friends for life. She may speak with pride of how different her children are from her and her husband, thanks to being schooled at Alpha Academy or St. George's College. Even those children who did not attain such scholastic and social heights speak Standard Jamaican English (learned in church and school, and fixed during their years of secondary education). Now they will be able to present themselves for positions such as bank tellers, nurses, accountants, and lawyers' clerks. In 1950, Mrs Chung's children were doing well. By this time, Mrs Chung herself is beginning to speak Standard Jamaican English, heavily accented, but clearly recognizable. She and I speak to one another in that version of Jamaican language, because she is an elder lady and sets the tone of conversation (and thus its linguistic form), while I am still the age of her youngest child.

I have searched and searched in my language repertoire and have never been able to find any dividing and determining rule *within languages themselves* to say how I should speak or write, save in social and cultural behaviour. The grammars of creole and of academic English do not tell me which to use, or why to use it. Yet each form carries loads of meaning that belong to it alone, just as French or Spanish carry each a universe of meaning which lives within the language itself. That is why we wretched speakers of English cannot easily use Spanish *ser* or *estar*. The tense system of English is far removed from the aspect system of Jamaican creole (try translating 'me done eat' into English), but we understand very well the meanings of each grammar.

All of this boils down to the fact that as children, we acquire a variety of language forms each marked for a cultural purpose, each defining a social role. We have varying skill in each form, depending on the household into which we are born, our schooling, and our contact with differing aspects of our society. Meaning exists in all of these forms: we do not get lost as we shift from patois to standard. We may indeed enjoy the shifting, using it for various effects and advantages. Yet because such shifts seldom occur in printed books, or in books that come from outside of our environment, we firmly believe that they have no place in the written word. Or rather, we have slowly and reluctantly — and then more eagerly and joyfully — accepted the fact that our language forms have as much right to be on the printed page as does metropolitan English.

As we all know, the use of any one of the available language forms carries with it a heavy weight of cultural, social, and political definition. We know that we assess one another by speech forms: every human group does so. Our assessments here in Jamaica possess more complexity and threat than many others because of our history, but we are far from being alone in our complicated language attitudes.

Why, for example, is this paper being written in standard English? It could be composed in basilectal form (Jamaican Creole or patois); in mesolectal form (Jamaican dialect shifted towards English grammar and vocabulary), in standard English, or, indeed a mix of all three. The choice of language form comes from the rules of our language behaviour. This is the form which I first heard used for formal discussions at home; for classes in school and Sunday school; and for stories that came from printed books. I obey the cultural rules here.

This is the language used in the novels which my mother read aloud to us — all six hundred pages of Victor Hugo's *Les Misérables*, [3] between 1942 and 1943. It must have taken about a year to get through it. The happenings in that novel were as vivid to me as if they were part of my family history. I was drawn inside the story, and its world fused into mine.

In about 1998, I read the book myself, for the first time. Somewhere around page 350, the voice in my head shifted abruptly from my own internal reading voice, and I heard *my mother's voice read half a paragraph*. It was so startling and strange that I stopped reading. How could this be, and she so long dead, since 1952? I read the lines again, but her voice was gone. Yet *her* voice forms the reality of that novel in my consciousness.

In those early days, the source of the story made no difference to me. Jean Valjean lived, as far as I was concerned, in Somerton, St. James. The pond where people were secretly drowned was in Somerton and in every novel. It was also in every poem. One chose the literary form to suit a particular audience and the kind of story. One could change the meaning of the story by changing the genre, as well as by shifting the language. That device was very handy for showing viewpoint, and with each viewpoint arises a new set of stories, new branches of meaning.

And all of the stories begin, for me, here in Jamaica, in the living language forms of Jamaica, in the voices of the narrator-audience. On the only occasion when I took the advice of an editor (an Englishman) and used the wrong kind of language — no creole, no dialect, and no shifts — the story died. *I could see the characters, but I could not hear them.* He had argued that an international audience would not want to bother with varieties of language from an obscure island. Another reader at this same press (Oxford University Press, ca. 1984) wondered why the novel should deal with anything as horrible as slavery, and why mention ship-brothers and ship-sisters? If I had wanted to test the relationship between me, my audience, and my language forms, I could not have taken a more definitive and disastrous step.

This experience was less than pleasurable, and made me wonder if stories were dead to me, but all it took to set off new vivid branches was meeting with children in Jamaica, and with friends whose vital stories charge me with energy and purpose. In the words of a former student who understands how our past informs all of our present doings, 'these narratives show, among other things, history at work in the construction of character, place, setting, even in the structures of emotion and feeling.... We Jamaicans are forever reckoning with the past, because, of course, the past is always present: the past works dynamically, not in a deterministic way'.[4] Thanks to the audience which renews me, and which I carry with me forever, I have been able to tell some of the stories in which I live, and move, and have my being.

Notes

1. Jean D'Costa, *Jenny and the General* (Kingston: Carlong Publishers, 2006).

2. Wilson Harris, *Palace of the Peacock* (London: Faber & Faber, [1960] 1988), 112, emphasis added.

3. Victor Hugo, *Les Misérables* [1862] (London: Penguin, 1982).

4. Veronica Gregg, personal communication.

Destination Smaddification

Amina Blackwood Meeks

Mawnin Boys and Girls, haspirants to Ladies and Genkklemanship, welcome aboard dis trip to Smaddification. We specifically welcome all dose who long to get on de Tourist Board, the Light and Power Board, de Communications Board but have no use fe de School Board. Is not your fault dem dont assign plenty money to heddication. You will be pleased to note that on this trip you will not be bored.

First we commence with a likkle introductions. My name is for me to know and you to find out. If you survive dis trip everybody will get to know your name. It will be on cocktail party invitation, building opening invitation, exhibition invitation, special commemoration invitation, and most of all who to leff off de invitation. For when yu turn into smaddy people delight in leffing yu off dem liss so dat you can see dat you is nat nobody. If you do not survive de chip, your name will not be known and you would never have been somebody and consequently nuh baddy wont have to dis yu by leffing yu off dem liss. Yu see it is not easy to reach destination smaddification.

Hongly people who are almost smaddy can teck dis tour. From dat state you shall be duly maddified. Dis is nat to say that you will get mad along de way. But if you do, you would have succeeded in reaching a higher level than most.

First you would observe that this is a walking tour. If at the end of it you are still walking, learn, know and understand that you have made it to the final destination. De first objective is to maddify you from walking to driving. Far when de credit union send man fe back yu up six o clock a mawnin and teck whey de car on account of your failure to meet de instalment, shame a go mad yu, dat mean yu is nat smaddy material and de adda people on de trip will vote yu off. Kinda like a likkle game show. So ef yu don't want people to teck yu life meck fun and joke, smaddification is nat far yu. Vote off yuself now. Tank yu sar, we will write yu when we reach.

Next ting. Dere are a few tings dat it is essential to have on this journey. A fair complexion. If yu do not have it abandon yu hopes of arriving at de destination now or run crass de wholesale and purchase yourself a bakkle of fast acting bleach.

Oops. Don't all push at once for memba dat a special team of police have been destroyed to kip arda. De badda you behave de arda dem lick yu. Arda! It is a requirement of smaddification dat some rule shud apply. Who it apply to is nat an issue. If yu bruk rule and get whey, you are on your way to being smaddified. Good. Now don't just hole de bleach bakkle in yu han maam, apply it!

You will learn tree tings on dis tour — what to drink, what to eat and what to drive. After dat you gane clear. De bleach, please. Careful doagh you could hen up with a disease called… fear of sunlight. But doan worry is nat you one have it. Disgraced bank managers, co-signers of car loans. We ongly exclude paliticians wid dere foot in dere mout. Decent people are equally afflicted.

Now, in addition to de bleach bakkle, you mus have anedda bakkle. Pan de outside mus have a label dat you cannot pronounce. Henybody who is anybady knows dat yu separate smaddy from haspirants to smaddy wid langwidge. Pan de inside now, sinting mussa a bubble. Dem who tink dem is smaddy have to pour it into glass and sip it slowly for bubbles will go hup into dem nose and cause dem harm. You now mus show dem who is really smaddy, tun de whole bakkle a yu head and gulp. Who, wha, money is no objeck and people cannot objeck to you when you have more money dan dem.

Dem might call yu hugly, dem might sey how yu look like Shabba, dem might sey yu kean tell glass from crystal, but dem want to be yu publicist, want yu in dem newspiapa and television screen, falla yu go a sunsplash fe get shocked by how much bad wud yu cuss. Yu large, yu is is smaddy, people talk about you.

Henybaddy hungry? We passing by a hotel where ladies an genkkleman serve ladies and genkklemen. Meck sure to eat tings dat people skin up dem nose afta. An nyam nuff a it. De likkle scraps a ting form out into a pattern and laas into a big oversize plate nah go work. And pay cash. Meck sure dem see dat yu billfold so full of bills, it kean fold. No debit card, no credit card, with your contacts yu nuh want nuh visa an yu a yu owna Master. And let them keep de change. Right dey so now yu know yu changing… more bleach. You can change into dem but dem kean change into you, you on your way up and dem nuh have no furder to go…. Das why dem is stretching out dem foot fe meck yu trip an fall. Who fah foot dat? Vote him off. Vote him off. Is awrite is inna him owna mout him put it.

You now are going to put your foot where everybaddy can see it, into a hupstairs kyar. Meck sure you choose de one wid a Escalator, or we have to vote you off de trip right here for lacking de ambition to climb up. While yu is climbing hup meck sure dem is coming down an permit dem to do it ongly once per week — Hot Monday, Crazy Tuesday, Weddy Wednesday, Passa Passa but dem can pass dere but once. You on de adda hand have to keep passing de bleach.

Going Bananas

come missa tallyman, tally me banana…

well, me nuh blame likkle miss jing bang. a dem wrang fe gane put har pan committee, an fe talk bout globalisation at dat.

me hear sey she turn up wid wan globe, slide projector, pitchas an wan dankey cart full a green banana. an she put awn a presentation dat meck farin dignitaries marvel.

de firs slide was a pretty barbar-green …

an she gi out:

dis is de road dat we buil

nex was a man wid him camera, miami vice shirt, wan likkle piecea sharts an wan grimace pan him face. dat was de touris who fraid fe walk pan de road dat we buil.

den she start go down de line. pitcha an narration.

dis is de hole dat cause de touris to fraid fe walk pan de road dat we buil

dis is de fire dat bun de hole dat cause de touris to fraid fe walk pan de road dat we buil

dis is de tyre dat ketch de fire dat bun de hole dat cause de touris to fraid fe walk pan de road dat we buil

dese are de people dat set de fire to de tyre dat bun de hole dat cause de touris fe fraid fe walk pan de road dat we buil outa har bag she produce what i hear cud only be described as some ole rusty ten-penny nail. an dose were de tacks dat juk de people dat set de fire to de tyre dat bun de hole dat cause de touris fe fraid fe walk pan de road dat we buil

dat cause everybaddi a scramble fe get a cuppa enyting an inna de rush wan a dem lick ova jing bang handbag, scatter whey all de likkle brown envelop wid de plastic window dat she had in dere.

massa. de bills we had to pay to prevent de tacks fram juk de people dat set de fire to de tyre dat bun de holes dat cause de touris to fraid fe de road dat we buil

den she pause an walk ova to har donkeycart full of green bananas. an every delegate get a sample meanwhile she a sing:

come missa tallyman, tally me banana,
daylight come an me waan go home...

an wen everybaddi hole a banana, hear har:

dese are de bananas we cud nat sell to get de money we had hoped to get to pay de bills to prevent de tacks from juk de people who set de fire to de tyre dat bun de hole dat cause de touris to fraid fe de roads dat we buil. so dem decide to travel by boat.

de nex slide de boat, dat wudden teck de bananas we cud nat sell to get an unnu hear areddi why we did want de money. but we neva had it an de touris en up fraid fe walk. so dem reques a travel advisory fram dem govament.

de govaments dat own de boats dat wudden teck de bananas we cud nat sell. an yu dun hear sey we did want de money.

but dem had a place, it name wto, where dem park de boats dat wudden teck de bananas we cud nat sell to get de money we had hoped to get to pay de bills to prevent de tacks, an yu dun know wen tacks juk people it hat like fire dat bun rubber tyre dat lead to nuff tings.

ah hear about a village where yu fine de place, wto, where dem park de boat dat wudden teck de bananas we cud nat sell to get de money we had hoped to get to pay de bills to avoid de tacks fram juk de people dat set fire to de tyre dat burn de hole dat cause de touris to fraid an run lef him camera.

ah hear him is someplace on dis globe where dem fine de village dat have de place, wto, to park de boats dat wudden teck de bananas. please to pass aroun de globe an see ef enywan can locate him.

den she produce some quality pictha wid people a trow stone an bakkle afta cricket umpire, man a run nakid fram mob inna port au prince, motorcade a meck nize pass sunday mawnin church service, people a marvel how rice truck know fe tun ova by itself right by fe dem gate...an she gi out:

dese are more people all ova de globe who goin bananas tryin to fine a way to stap dose tings dat cause de touris fe fraid fe walk pan de road dat we buil.

an den she bow. an dat, ladies an genkklemen is globalization.

day, me say day, me say day, me say day oh
day light come an me wan go home
come missa tallyman, tally me banana
daylight come an me waan go home...

The Writer in the Caribbean Language Situation

MERLE HODGE

Part of what 'writing life' entails, in our part of the world, is treating with a language situation which for the writer is a rich resource, but also a distinct challenge. For as long as there has been written fiction coming out of the Anglophone Caribbean, writers have taken on board the fact of language variety as a feature of the society. Most West Indian writers of fiction have found it necessary to engage in one way or another with the first language of their community, so that the appearance of Creole on the page is a long-standing Caribbean tradition — still occasionally challenged by the anti-'broken-English' brigade, but here to stay. There are, however, issues to do with the written representation of this language that are worthy of our attention if we are committed to continually improving our craft. West Indian writers of fiction experience challenges with the transcribing of Creole in each of the dimensions of the language — lexicon, phonology, and grammar.

Although the language of our part of the region is described as 'English-lexicon' Creole, we do have considerable inputs of vocabulary from other languages, as well as words coined afresh by our speech communities, and English words which have undergone semantic shifts. Trinidadian Creole (TC), for example, because of its multi-ethnic background, has a particularly rich infusion of non-English lexicon, its sources being French-lexicon Creole, Hindi-Bhojpuri, West African languages, Amerindian languages, Spanish, and others. Thus far, however, that part of the TC lexical stock is only sparsely represented in the written fiction of Trinidad and Tobago, presumably because of the risk of locking out non-Trinidadian readers, even other West Indian readers, since each of our societies has its own set of non-English lexical items. The publication of Allsopp's *Dictionary of Caribbean English*[1] may well empower writers to more freely use the lexicon that is specific to our various speech communities.

Resources are also available to address the challenges encountered by writers in their efforts to represent Creole phonology. We are faced with the task of capturing the sounds of Creole by the use of a spelling system that was devised long ago and far away for another language — Standard English (SE) orthography, itself quite inconsistent and a misfit in relation to modern SE.

Based on a perception that the essence of Creole resides in the sound of it, some new writers, for example participants in creative writing workshops and classes, may perform elaborate modifications to SE spelling in order to write Creole. The end product, referred to by linguists as 'eye dialect' is discussed, rather scathingly, by Peter Roberts in *West Indians and their Language*:

> [It] is an idiosyncratic orthography or an alteration of a partially phonetic orthography to make it more phonetic by people who generally have little knowledge of linguistic phonetics.[2]

Many writers-in-the-making seem to feel, passionately, that the language is somehow betrayed or disrespected if the distinctiveness of its phonology is not acknowledged. One might also observe that many of our established writers have made more use of eye dialect in their first novels than in their later works. A statement made by Samuel Selvon on the subject of phonetic spelling is certainly not applicable to his first novel, *A Brighter Sun*:

> One of the things I have always assiduously avoided is to write, to spell words phonetically. I feel that this jars on the readers' eyes and it makes any dialect form so much more difficult to understand.[3]

Earl Lovelace's first novel *While Gods Are Falling* also displays a high incidence of phonetic spelling compared to his subsequent fiction. And I encounter with alarm, in *Crick Crack, Monkey*,[4] some of the spelling practices that today I discourage in creative writing students.

Writing Creole is not a case of recording every single feature of Creole pronunciation in every single word of written Creole. That would be a hopeless enterprise, for, as we are reminded by Barbara Lalla in her piece 'Creole Representation in Literary Discourse':

> representation of the Creole in literature can never actually be realistic, any more than any scribal representation of oral discourse can be more than impressionistic. Creole features may be included with accuracy ... but can hardly be maintained with rigorous precision.[5]

Over-zealous deforming of SE spelling produces certain problems. It makes reading Creole an uphill task, for SE as well as Creole speakers, since our word recognition skills are also developed in relation to English phonics and the physical shapes, on the page, of individual English words. Another disadvantage is that some of the alterations to SE spelling undermine the independence and the validity of Creole. For example, the practice of placing apostrophes to indicate what are perceived to be 'missing' sounds, characterizes the language as broken, incomplete — English with omissions. Features of SE that do not appear in Creole cannot be considered missing, because Creole is not English.

Most writers feel some need to establish that Creole sounds different from SE, or to ensure that the reader knows when the text has shifted into Creole even though on the page it might look like SE. Writers sometimes also mark phonology to indicate differences between the registers or varieties of Creole used by their characters. However, the representation of Creole phonology in our writing actually only amounts to flagging — a token selection of features highlighted only some of the time. For example, in one continuous passage of Creole a writer might indicate the Creole progressive aspect ending by rendering it as *in* once or twice, but spell it *ing* the nine other times that the speaker uses it. This does not mean that the speaker switches nine times into SE pronunciation.

Individual writers tend to have a favoured set of Creole sounds that they seem to consider important to the specificity of the language, and may never, or seldom, give any focus at all to other salient parts of its phonology. For example, some writers signal the Creole speaker's use of the sounds [d] and [t] where SE uses [ð] and [ɵ], and some choose not to.

The flagging of phonology is a perfectly acceptable literary strategy. Indeed, it is the only option in our present circumstances; and certainly there can be no suggestion of an imposed orthodoxy regarding which sounds a writer chooses to represent. My concern is with the method of representation, when one does choose to signal Creole phonology. The body of written literature that West Indian writers have produced to date presents a picture of entirely individualistic and unstable methods of writing what is fundamentally the same language even when one takes into consideration the details of country-to-country variation.

A poignant illustration of the challenges of writing Creole is provided by the array of Trinidadian writers' attempts at representing three words that are used so frequently in everyday communication in TC that, in the enterprise of writing Trinidadian life, they cannot be avoided. These are the preverbal negators [dō] (from *don't*) and [ɛ̃]/[ẽ] (from *ain't*), and the negative verb [kjã] (from *can't*). The problem is that they each contain a nasalized vowel, unaccompanied by a nasal consonant. English spelling makes no provision for this phenomenon, so how to write these unavoidable function words? Taken together, the range of writers' attempts conjures up an image of floundering. [dō] is rendered as *do', doh, don, doan, dohn* and *don't*. [ɛ̃]/[ẽ], may be *eh, ehn, ehnt, en, ain', ent, in,* or *ain't*. Among the spellings offered for [kjã] are: *cyar, cyah, kean, kean't, kian't, kyar, kyah, carn', carn't,* or *can't*. And in the course of one novel, short story, or paragraph, a writer may freely switch from one spelling to another of the same word. Another example is the range of variants for the spelling of the second person pronoun. The singular, possessive form may be spelt *you, yer, yuh, yu, yo, your,* or *you'*. The plural form of the second person, in TC, appears as *allyuh, allyu, all-you,* or *all you*.

There may seem to be little point, at this stage, of seeking to standardize the orthography of Creole, when West Indian fiction has fared so well in the world of literature, notwithstanding its unsystematic methods of representing its own language. However, the absence of norms in the written form of Creole can create an impression of arbitrariness, of makeshift — hardly the image of a solid, respected cultural institution.[6] And what the international audience thinks about our language is not half as important as how Creole speakers see Creole. West Indian writers should consider moving towards some consensus regarding a common strategy for the representation of Creole phonology in fiction.

Standardized orthographies exist for the anglophone and francophone Creoles of the Caribbean. The problem is their institutionalization. Frederic Cassidy's definitive edition of the writing system which he developed, 'A Revised Phonemic Orthography for Anglophone Caribbean Creoles', was published almost thirty years ago (1978).[7] To my knowledge, writers of fiction have so far shown no interest in it, and are unlikely to adopt any such change in one fell swoop. Mervyn Morris suggests, in his essay 'Printing the Performance',[8] that the ground may have to be prepared by its introduction into formal education, as proposed by Hubert Devonish.[9] Such a development, however, is hardly imminent. Our Ministries of Education are far more conservative than writers, so it may well happen the other way around, that writers eventually lead the way to acceptance of a linguistically sound writing system for Creole. Meanwhile, the reality, deftly summarized by Mervyn Morris, is that:

> most of us have chosen compromise. The most common (if inconsistent) approach is to write the vernacular for the eye accustomed to Standard English, but with various alterations signalling Creole.[10]

It is not uncommon for the preface to a West Indian literary text to carry an explication of a specific compromise regarding orthography, consciously and carefully worked out by writer or editor. Morris's essay 'Printing the Performance' sets out one such process, quoted from his preface to Louise Bennett's *Selected Poems*.[11] V.S. Naipaul, in the foreword to his father's collection of short stories *The Adventures of Gurudeva*, [12] gives a rationale for his editing of the Creole dialogue written by the senior Naipaul. Honor Ford-Smith, scribe and editor of the collection of narratives *Lionheart Gal: Life Stories of Jamaican Women*, also outlines a studied approach to the transcribing of Creole that combines different systems. She describes the strategy used in this work as 'a compromise between phonetic spelling, English spelling and spellings which have become commonly accepted through constant usage'. [13]

Other writers have worked out different compromises, or have settled, comfortably or not, into what can only be compromise for as long as we do not adopt a standardized orthography specifically designed for Creole phonology. While we wait, or work towards universal acceptance of proper standardization, could we not hammer out a standardized compromise? This could be achieved at a writers' workshop facilitated in part by linguists, or a series of workshops spread over a period that accommodates a timetable for widespread consultation with, and experimentation by, the writers.

There is another observation to be made on the topic of phonology that applies also to the representation of Creole grammar in our writing. The examples I give will again be from Trinidadian fiction.

Among the variants of spelling for the TC negator [ɛ̃]/[ɛ̃], the one that Trinidadian writers opt for most frequently is *ain't*, a feature of British and American non-standard dialects, and therefore familiar to international readers of literature in English. Next, the SE sound [ɜ], as in *first, work* and *burst*, has as its counterpart in the variety of TC that is furthest from SE (basilectal TC), the vowel [ɔ]: *fos, wok, bos*. Another variant is [o]: *foce, woke, boce*. In intermediate varieties of TC, this sound becomes [ʌ] (*fus, wuk, bus*); but the basilectal versions are alive and well in a wide band of Trinidadian speech, and in oral literary genres such as calypso, rapso, storytelling and drama. Interestingly, however, when Trinidadian writers choose to signal that basilectal speakers have an alternative pronunciation to SE [ʌ], they commonly resort to [ʌ], rather than [ʌ]/[o]; that is, they more often spell it with a *u* than with an *o*. The [ʌ] would be characteristic of the variety of Creole spoken by people exposed to a longer process of education than others, and writers tend to fall into that category. On the other hand, the replacement of [ɜ] by [ʌ] also occurs to a limited extent in British and American non-standard English, in specific words such as *bust* and *cuss*, for example, variants of *burst* and *curse*.

The SE diphthong [ou] (*ow*), when it is followed by the nasal vowel *n*, is replaced, in TC, by [oŋ] (*ong*). For example, the English words *down*, *town* and *pound* are, in TC, *dong*, *tong* and *pong*. To say 'downtown' with SE pronunciation, in ordinary, everyday conversation, whoever you are, would seem extremely affected. The *ong* sound in this syllable is entrenched and widespread in intermediate as well as basilectal varieties of Trinidadian speech. Yet it is not a phonological feature of Creole that Trinidadian writers have considered it essential to flag. I have so far seen it represented only by one of the writers I surveyed, and featured only very sparingly, at that.

These examples from the realm of phonology fit into a general pattern of writers apparently trimming away, in their literary representation of Creole, features that are furthest away from SE. The trend is also found in their representation of Creole grammar. Some basic traditional forms of TC grammar are being edged out of written fiction by forms closer to SE — mesolectal forms. And again, it is not that the basilectal forms in question no longer have currency in the Trinidadian speech community. The linguists would argue that the trend in literature simply reflects the death or dying of the basilect in Trinidad; but the Creole forms that Trinidadian writers seem to be forsaking are alive and well in contemporary Trinidadian speech. They feature in one or another of the rich complex of varieties that together constitute active Creole today. An examination of pronoun usage will alone suffice as illustration.

In the original structure of the Anglophone Caribbean Creoles, personal pronouns are not inflected for case as obtains in SE. One form functions as subject, object, and possessive adjective. For some pronouns the form most commonly selected for all of these functions is the SE object form: *me, them, him*. In nineteenth-century Trinidadian fiction, Creole-speaking characters consistently use *me* in the subject position;[14] but today *me* has largely been replaced, in TC, by *I*, more usually pronounced [a] or [ʌ], with [ai] reserved for stressed positions. Yet *me* as subject has by no means disappeared from TC. It survives as an alternative form, specifically when the verb — usually a stative verb — is used with the negator [ɛ̃]/[ẽ]:

'Me eh tink dat Pandit go do dat.' [15] (Ladoo)

This is not a quaint and dying retention found only in pockets of the rural landscape. Its use is widespread and tenacious, but the structure is hard to find in twentieth-century Trinidadian fiction.[16] This is also the fate of the pronoun *dem* as subject, which in real life is still an option alongside a shift to *dey*.

The SE nominative forms *he*, *she*, and *we* are the ones used for all the cases in what might be classified as the basilectal part of TC. Their use for the object and possessive functions is represented in written fiction:

'...he have to find out what work make for he'.[17] (Khan)

'I didn't tell you that she nearly throw sheself away for nothing?'[18] (Lovelace)

'He keant see what in we pot, chile.'[19] (de Boissière)

However, the high incidence of the equivalent SE forms, *him, his, her, us,* and *our,* in Trinidadian literature does not seem to reflect their actual distribution in everyday speech. The two systems of pronoun usage coexist in the repertoire of TC speakers, who may switch between the two in the stream of speech; and in the everyday language of a significant sector of the population, the traditional system is predominant. This, however, is one of the habits of Creole that disappear from our Creole repertoire as we proceed up the scale of education or social class.

The voice of Lovelace's narrator, Eva, in *The Wine of Astonishment*, is a good example of the apparent shift, in the Creole of Trinidadian fiction, towards the register used by people with relatively advanced education. Eva has the social profile of a Trinidadian who, especially in the 1940s, the era in which the novel is set, would speak a Creole with a higher incidence of basilectal forms than one finds in the narration of this work. Her choice of pronouns, for example, is overwhelmingly SE, with only a sprinkling of utterances such as 'the police in we tail'.[20]

One question is whether West Indian writers of fiction inadvertently impose their own speech patterns on their characters, or whether they consciously edit out features of Creole that they see as likely to alienate, or irritate, or disorient the English-speaking reader. Is this unwitting transference, or calculated concession to the external audience? That is another discussion. A concern that I would like to put forward is, rather, to do with the possible impact of 'literary Creole' — especially where the writer, in addition to selecting the grammatical forms closest to SE, makes no concession whatsoever to Creole phonology, so that 'Creole' becomes visually almost indistinguishable from SE. There is the likelihood that the literary variety of Creole will take on a prestige that causes it to be seen as 'standard' Creole, more acceptable than the varieties which retain traditional features. Such a development could hasten the process identified by some linguists as 'decreolization',[21] and that, for me, would not be a desirable outcome.

Hubert Devonish, even as he advocates the use of Creole as an official language, warns against 'imposing a single variety of Creole on everyone in the society'.[22] The development of a sanitized version of Creole, as the form that appears in books, would be one means by which this bleak prospect could materialize.

It is time that the years of work carried out in the field of Creole linguistics be put to greater use in the literary field. There are three groups that need to have more concrete, more scientific knowledge of the language: writers using Creole as a medium; literary critics analysing West Indian literature; and publishers who edit West Indian literature.

I have had the experience of writers — skilful and accomplished writers — asking me to read a piece of work that they have written with Creole in it, because they have been agonizing over whether it is really Creole, whether it is good Creole, that rings true, and so on. As a normal part of their education, French writers, English writers, Danish writers reflect upon the structure of their language, that which is the medium of their craft. We speak ours and we hear it around us, but our knowledge of it remains fuzzy. We have no analytical perspective on our first language.

Today, linguistics has found its way into West Indian literary criticism. Serious analytic attention has been given to the dimension of language in our literature by scholars such as Jean D'Costa, Maureen Warner-Lewis, Barbara Lalla, Velma Pollard, Mervyn Morris, Carolyn Cooper and Lise Winer. Traditionally critics would dish up the Creole part of a literary text by characterizing it superficially as a 'flavour', or a 'tone' — something nebulous that they were unable to conceptualize in precise terms. Another phenomenon is the non-West Indian literary critic who makes erroneous judgements of a text that reveal his/her lack of competence in Creole. (The work of Samuel Selvon, for example, has attracted both types.) There are also cases of editors in publishing houses abroad tampering with written Creole in manuscripts and thereby distorting the intended meaning, or simply producing incorrect Creole.

A great deal of knowledge has been generated about our language and our language situation. All of us who are involved, in one way or another, in the work of developing West Indian literature would do well to equip ourselves with the fundamentals of this knowledge. This I see as related to the larger project of developing Caribbean cultural confidence through expanding Caribbean self-knowledge.

Notes

1. Richard Allsopp, *The Dictionary of Caribbean English Usage, with a French and Spanish Supplement* (Oxford: Oxford University Press, 1996).
2. Peter A. Roberts, *West Indians and their Language* (Cambridge: Cambridge University Press, 1988), 137.
3. Peter Nazareth, 'Interview with Sam Selvon', *World Literature Written in English* 18.2 (1979): 421–22. See also Samuel Selvon, *A Brighter Sun* [1952] (London: Longman, 1971).
4. Merle Hodge, *Crick Crack, Monkey* [1970] (London: Heinemann, 1981).
5. Barbara Lalla, 'Creole Representation in Literary Discourse: Issues of Linguistic and Discourse Analysis' in *Exploring the Boundaries of Caribbean Creole Languages*, eds. Hazel Simmons-McDonald and Ian Robertson (Kingston: University of the West Indies Press, 2006).

6. Winford James also links the standardization of orthography to righting the image and status of Creole (Winford James and Valerie Youssef, *The Languages of Tobago: Genesis, Structure and Perspectives*, St. Augustine: University of the West Indies School of Continuing Studies, 2002, 198–204).

7. Frederic Cassidy, 'A Revised Phonemic Orthography for Anglophone Caribbean Creoles' (Proceedings of the Conference of the Society for Caribbean Linguistics. Cave Hill, Barbados, University of the West Indies, 1978).

8. Mervyn Morris, '*Is English We Speaking' and Other Essays* (Kingston: Ian Randle Publishers, 1999), 46–47.

9. Hubert Devonish, *Language and Liberation* (London: Karia Press, 1986), 114.

10. Mervyn Morris, '*Is English We Speaking*', 47.

11. Ibid., 48. See also Louise Bennett, *Selected Poems* (Kingston: Sangster's, 1982).

12. Seepersad Naipaul, *The Adventures of Gurudeva* (London: Heinemann, 1995).

13. Honor Ford-Smith, ed. with the Sistren Collective, *Lionheart Gal: Life Stories of Jamaican Women* (London: The Women's Press, 1986), xxix.

14. In texts such as E.L. Joseph's *Warner Arundell, The Adventures of a Creole*, ed. Lise Winer [1838] (Kingston: University of the West Indies Press, 2001) and Maxwell Philip's *Emmanuel Appadoca: or, Blighted Life* (Port of Spain: Mole Brothers, 1854; Amherst: University of Massachusetts Press, 1997).

15. Harold Sonny Ladoo, *Yesterdays* (Toronto: Anansi, 1974), 28.

16. The work of Sonny Ladoo features a number of traditional Creole forms eschewed by other writers.

17. Ismith Khan, *The Jumbie Bird* (London: Longman, 1974), 160.

18. Earl Lovelace, *While Gods are Falling* [1965] (Harlow: Longman, 1984), 88.

19. Ralph de Boissière, *Crown Jewel* [1952] (London: Picador, 1981), 80.

20. Earl Lovelace, *The Wine of Astonishment* [1982] (London: Heinemann, 1986), 1.

21. For example, John A. Holm, *Pidgins and Creoles*, 2 vols. (Cambridge: Cambridge University Press, 1988), 9.

22. Hubert Devonish, *Language and Liberation*, 115.

The Reluctant Interpreter

OLIVE SENIOR

I would like to acknowledge the major role played by the University of the West Indies (UWI) in creating the climate in which an indigenous literature could take root and flourish.

Let me start by sharing with you the path I took to be a writer and some of the unforeseen requirements that I encountered along the way. I would then like to discuss what I see as my role as a West Indian writer.

At an early age I decided I was going to be a writer. Of course I didn't know what that really meant, I had no role model and no concept. I did have this vision of myself sitting in splendid isolation and writing words that I would then send forth into the world. I had no idea that there were so many other components to consider, including the fact that I as the author would be expected to accompany these words into the world.

Imagine my shock to discover after the publication of my first books that there was a public expectation about the writer that also had to be satisfied. I now feel able to confess the shameful episode of my first public reading. It was here at UWI, organized by Dr Victor Chang as part of a series. I was too shy to read so I begged Eddie Baugh and Velma Pollard to do so for me and they read my work to the audience, while I sat there, quaking. My next reading, I remember, was shortly afterwards at Bolivar Gallery with Lorna Goodison, and this time I managed it, probably because it was a much smaller space and audience.

The fact that I don't remember subsequent readings with equal clarity will tell you that I was forced to overcome my fear. But in this and other ways I discovered early in my career that it is not just about the writing. Nowadays, more than ever, the expectation is that the writer's persona will be part of the equation. Especially now in the era of market-driven publishing, some writers are stars — or think they are.

The writer is seen as part of a package whether as physical presence or as embodied in the writing. We as writers can glibly say we 'write for ourselves', but that self has a history that is enmeshed in society, and all of this is revealed in whatever we chose to write. Writing in whatever form is self-exposure, so the reader should be able to extract from the work something of the persona and personal ideology of the writer, no matter how disguised.

If I had the choice, I would still prefer to leave the persona out of the equation and have only my written words to speak for me. It is still a shock sometimes to realize that people regard what I do as 'special' and the writer as some sort of oracle. Equally shocking is the fact that there are still too many people who have no regard for what I do for, after all, anyone can be a writer. Or so it is believed by those people — more numerous than you think — who say, when they realize I am a writer, 'Oh, I would write too, if I had the time.' Clearly, there are still many who fail to recognize that, at a basic level, writing is a job of work like any other, though often a largely unpaid one.

I was a published writer for a long time before I realized there were additional factors to consider. For instance, there is curiosity about the whole process of writing. I began as an intuitive writer — I still am — by which I mean that I have an innate sense of what is required, and also that I learnt to write from reading, not from attending classes.

But once you are published you are forced to think of the whole process of writing and what it entails because you get asked these questions about the process by interviewers, audiences, students, academics. And in my case once I started teaching writing then I had to think of all the technical challenges of the craft as well as the wider philosophical issues. For instance: Why was I doing what I was doing? Had I chosen it or had it chosen me?

I am still not sure of the answers. Clearly, I have been assigned a role, but sometimes I don't know whose play I am in and I can't see much of the audience. Which is very different from the deterministic view of one's work that is taught today in academia, that is, that the writer has motive.

Finally, there is the business side of writing. This is another element for the writer to learn, one that becomes more difficult, not easier as you go along, for this concerns what happens to the work once you have completed it. Getting the publisher for your work which then becomes a 'product', the marketing and selling of it. Some people are much better at this than others, because in today's competitive world this can also be interpreted as selling yourself. And the big question remains, do you want to? It depends on how hungry you are. Writers who live outside the Caribbean might be seen to have an easier time of it, but that brings its own problematic. Because if your work is still rooted in the Caribbean it becomes more and more difficult to sell to a publisher outside. And often the writer is forced to make choices about what to write to be successful or even to be published. If you don't choose to write about your adopted home or the themes that are the current staples of metropolitan publishing, for instance, themes of 'exile' or 'displacement', then *dog nyam your supper*.

The business of writing of course is even harder in the Caribbean where there are lots of publishers and good ones too, but no sustained initiative to publish what we might call 'creative work' — novels and short fiction, poetry and plays. In a country such as Canada writing now flourishes because of government recognition of the importance of the arts to the development of national identity and the need to provide for its sustenance through public support of writers and publishing. No such initiative exists in the Caribbean, as far as I know. Yet few national literatures can really flourish without such public support.

I am frequently asked the question: 'for whom do you write?' My answer has always been: for anyone. Because I truly believe that my writing should be universally understood even though some of the cultural context and even some of the language and other nuances might be lost to those who are not from my country of origin. At the same time, I am conscious of writing out of a sense of place. In a sense that place also determines who my primary readers are: the people of Jamaica and the wider Caribbean.

The next question: What is your role as a writer? My role as a writer is simply to do the best job I can. And that means doing an honest job of interpretation and representation. It is also about fulfilling the expectation of the other. Of you, Dear Reader.

I think what we really do as writers is fill a niche. Like all other artists, we provide the expression for people's dreams. We ferret out desires and try to express them in whatever way we can. Most people, especially in today's material culture, are primarily concerned with what Marshall McLuhan calls 'learning a living'. Few have the opportunity or the willingness to stand back and assess what is going on around them; to contextualize themselves. It is the artist's job, I think, to take this journey beyond everyday reality, to stand at the 'still point of the turning world', to look, listen, learn, and find our way back with something to say about the experience that will strike a chord for the reader, viewer or listener. This is what I call 'interpretation' and why I see myself as an 'interpreter', albeit a reluctant one.

My referring to the writer as 'interpreter' might seem pretentious, even impertinent. Who gave me that authority or qualification? But here I am merely using 'interpreter' to mean not so much 'one who translates' as one who is an agent or broker, one who gives a solution or answer to a question. For questions, and the need to find things out, are the raw material of the writer's trade. All art begins with questions about experience. The writer experiences then interrogates — in other words, asks questions — and then shares both the questions and answers with the reader or viewer or listener (note that I do not say the 'consumer' although I know that art is a commodity and the poem, story or book is the writer's way of packaging his or her experience). I believe that that experience which is expressed in the work, the writing, should be of such substance as to have some impact on the reader. Which is why I'm fond of a saying attributed to Gauguin that 'Art is either plagiarism or revolution.'

Near where I live in downtown Toronto there is a small outdoor sculpture garden and every time I walk through I am amused by the notice that says: 'Please be advised that contact with the art work is at the user's own risk'. I suppose this is because there are constantly changing exhibits, some of which might jump out and bite you. Which is what I think all art should aim to do — metaphorically speaking of course — leave you in an emotionally breathless state. It should at the very least elicit an emotional response — shock, awe, or amazement. If writing begins with an emotional response on the part of the writer to something apprehended through the senses, the end result should be an emotional response from the reader. This is where the connection takes place.

The answers to questions that one gets from art are not necessarily the answers one seeks in daily life. As individuals we focus on what is happening at each moment of our lives and these events are what we deal with on an everyday basis. The writer's job is to go beyond individual experiences to try and frame our questions and our work within a broader perspective. In other words, even as we write about the singular life we are presenting Life — with a capital L — in all its verisimilitude — as joy, pain, hate, betrayal, love, treachery, kindness, and so on. Art therefore allows the individual to fit the events of his or her own life into a broader matrix. Through identification with characters, events, plots, poetic images and so on, the reader might recognize not only answers but questions he or she never thought to ask in her time of need. Through art, individuals can see the possibility for heroism in their daily lives. Heroism not just as action but as the acquisition of the ability to arrive at solutions, the revelation of 'the world in a grain of sand'. Insight itself is heroic.

The raw material of writing is experience — any and all kinds of experience, however acquired. Yet the writer's only tool is language. The writer has a duty to use language in a caring and truthful way for only then will it retain its freshness, its power to please, amaze, or shock. For although I have said the writer must place individual experience within a general social matrix, the paradox is that we write about the general through the eyes of the singular individual. Thus the challenge is to particularize the universal: to speak of large events through small mouths. The employment of language in a general way debases it so that it loses its meaning — as we all know, for instance, from the experience of, say, political rhetoric which usually seems contrived from a template.

Finally, the question might be asked: *how does one go about the task of interpretation?* I would say the task is not so much concerned with the known as with the unknown — the terrain waiting to be explored. Thus our exploration of home, the place that gives impetus to our art, is not that 'home is where the heart is'; it is the place where the heart is not. Wandering in that unknown terrain in order to acquire the necessary perspective is the writer's mandate or duty. To do so, the writer has to reject complacency, conformity, comfort or the template, separate him or herself from the known, in psychological terms, and find her way back home. And the thread that leads one back home becomes the writing itself which is inexhaustible, like Anansi's magic thread. For the more one writes, the greater the acquisition of what I'll simply call 'story' to encompass all the literary forms. As we know, all stories are owned by Anansi. And no story stands on its own as something isolated or singular. All stories have their pedigree, they are thread in a huge family web that weaves back and forth through history, through time, through space, and from the underworld to the celestial sphere. It is the writer's duty to follow these threads wherever they lead for nothing that we do exists in isolation. Through the threads of our stories embedded in fiction or poetry or drama, we provide the opportunity for our audience, our reader, to link his or her personal story (the particular) to the larger one being presented (the universal web).

I call myself a 'reluctant' interpreter because I would like to go back to that role in which I cast myself as a small child, that of the distanced creator. And yet, even this 'reluctance' is part of our West Indian story, for resistance is embedded in the mythology of who we are as a people. That is, just being difficult. Difficulty that is rooted in ambivalence, the push-pull factors that govern us.

To be a writer is a solo act, yet the creative self needs nourishment the same as the other selves. Part of this nourishment comes from the outside world — the people who read us and praise us and appreciate what we do (and, it goes without saying, who buy our books!). Yet an essential part of that nourishment, that preparation for the journey, is the retreat into intentional solitude, a situation that I think of as being 'islanded'. For the island more than anything else is the symbol of that solitude. Not our island of course in which we 'disturb our neighbours' every night, but the island of the mind — the desert island evoking sanctuary or refuge from the waves. 'No man is an island', nor is the remotest island unaffected by the push and pull of nature. Born of the sea, each island remains at the mercy of the sea, which wears it down and builds it up, even as it is colonized by flora or fauna. So even as we plunge into the solitary self, the sea of the unconscious awaits us to nourish us for our reintegration into the wider world.

Does one write for the public good or for oneself? I certainly don't think the writer should consciously assume responsibility for 'the public good' or 'for society' — that is not the writer's role. We speak for ourselves. Yet that self is inseparable from a public. Whether we write for the public good or not is a choice each writer has to make and not necessarily in a conscious way. As I said earlier, all of our work, no matter what the subject matter, is in some way revealing of the writer's world view and personal ideology. Perhaps, to conclude, we might attempt to place some of the choices available to the writer within the context of some expressions of Jamaican mythology:

(1) Do we want to be 'Warner Woman' who gets signals from the spirit world and goes about announcing apocalyptic images of death and destruction, disturbing people but not offering much in the way of solution?

(2) Do we want to be 'Ribba Mumma' or a guardian of the Golden Table, selling our individual soul for untold riches or maybe just for one night of bliss?

(3) Do we want to be 'Rolling Calf', 'Three Foot Horse' or any monster that initially terrifies but can be easily defeated by a tarred whip, a low fence, or incantations by the knowledgeable?

(4) Or do we want to see ourselves as the original web-master, 'Anansi'? Not the debased Anansi, the samfi man of the Caribbean, but Anansi the trickster and creative genius who organizes chaos in order to generate change, who seriously wants to disturb the neighbour, and who warns the user of the risk of consuming our stories.

Just as Anansi spins its web out of its own substance, what we should be doing as writers is not worrying about our 'role' but about creating from the fabric of our experiences stories, poems, plays that are so honest, so true, so joyous, so heartrending, that you the consumer should indeed become mesmerized and enmeshed. Contact definitely at the user's own risk.

Contributors

Kevin Baldeosingh is the author of three novels, *The Autobiography of Paras P* (1996), *Virgin's Triangle* (1997) and *The Ten Incarnations of Adam Avatar* (2005). He was regional chairperson (Canada/Caribbean) for the Commonwealth Writers Prize (2000 and 2001). He is a founding member of the Trinidad and Tobago Humanist Association. He has worked for all three daily Trinidad and Tobago newspapers as a columnist, feature writer and editorial writer. At present, he works for the Trinidad *Newsday* as a specialist writer on a freelance basis.

Amina Blackwood Meeks, who was born in Jamaica, lived and worked in Guyana and the Eastern Caribbean for more than fourteen years. A UWI Social Sciences graduate, she is also a trained early childhood educator, a newspaper columnist, an actor and a storyteller. She helped to create the Caribbean Storytelling Festival in Barbados, Gimistory in Cayman and LikkleStoryFest in Jamaica. Audio-cassettes of her work include *in the tropics*, *Once Upon a Time...Is Now* and *Invocation*. Whether performing on stage, or teaching at the Edna Manley College or working with community-based organizations, she has found the persona and skills of the storyteller useful in connecting ancient values with modern needs. She is currently pursuing graduate work in Cultural Studies.

Erna Brodber is Jamaican. She holds postgraduate degrees in sociology and history. She was employed at the University of the West Indies, but since 1985 has been making her living as a visiting professor. Her books of fiction are *Jane and Louisa Will Soon Come Home* (1980), *Myal* (1988), *Louisiana* (1994) and *The Rainmaker's Mistake* (2007). *Myal* was chosen as the Canada/Caribbean region best book in competition for the 1989 Commonwealth Prize. Dr Brodber has published several articles and ten books (two are collaborations) in sociology and history, the most recent being *Standing Tall* (2003), *The Continent of Black Consciousness* (2003), *The Second Generation of Freemen in Jamaica* (2004) and *Woodside, Peartree Grove P.O.* (2004). She is the recipient of a Musgrave Gold Medal, Jamaica's Order of Distinction (Commander Class) and the Prince Claus Award from the Kingdom of the Netherlands.

Alwin Bully, who was born in Dominica, has worked in a number of cultural activities. Actor, theatre director, designer, playwright, composer, painter, he is an administrator also. At the UWI Cave Hill campus, where he earned a BA degree, he was president of the Guild of Undergraduates and helped to start the Cave Hill Drama Society, the Cavite Chorale and the Cave Hill carnival. Returning home, he taught at the Dominica Grammar School and became headmaster at the age of 27. In 1977 he was appointed to establish the Government Department of Culture, of which he was the first director. He served as manager of Dominica Broadcasting Services in 1980. In 1987 he joined UNESCO and moved to Jamaica as senior programme specialist/adviser for culture in the Caribbean. Especially as a director and a designer, he has also been active in Jamaican theatre. He has won several regional and international awards.

Staceyann Chin, a Jamaican resident in New York City, was co-writer and performer in the Tony Award winning *Russell Simmons Def Poetry Jam* on Broadway. She burst into public view with a series of Poetry Slam awards beginning in 1998. Since then she has performed and conducted workshops in the United States, Denmark and London. She has been featured on cable and radio, and been received with acclaim at the Nuyorican Poets' Cafe and in one-woman shows off-Broadway, including *Hands Afire* (2000), *Unspeakable Things* (2001) and *Border/Clash* (2005). Her writings have appeared in many publications in the United States, including the *Shades Newsletter*, *GMAD* magazine, the *New York Times*, the *Washington Post* and the *Pittsburg Daily*.

Merle Collins, who is from Grenada, studied at the UWI, Mona, and in the United States and England. She teaches Creative Writing and Caribbean Literature at the University of Maryland. Her publications include two novels, *Angel* (1987), *The Colour of Forgetting* (1995); a book of short stories, *Rain Darling* (1990); and three poetry collections, *Because the Dawn Breaks* (1985), *Rotten Pomerack* (1990), and *Lady in a Boat* (2003). In 1995 she completed for BBC Radio a programme titled 'From Africa to the Caribbean: A Journey of the Oral Tradition'. She has been working on a project entitled *From Africa to the Caribbean: A Study of Village Traditions in Grenada*. Her awards include a Guggenheim Fellowship.

Kwame Dawes was born in Ghana in 1962 but grew up in Jamaica, where he attended Jamaica College and the University of the West Indies. After studies in New Brunswick he moved to the United States in 1992. He is Louise Frye Liberal Arts Professor in the College of Liberal Arts and Distinguished Poet in Residence at the University of Southern Carolina. He is criticism editor for *Obsidian III*, poetry editor for Peepal Tree Press, and programmer for the Calabash International Literary Festival. His books of poetry include *Progeny of Air* (1994) and *Midland* (2001) which won prizes, *New and Selected Poems* (2003) and *Impossible Flying* (2007). He is the author of many plays, including *One Love* (2001). His other publications include a collection of short stories, *A Place to Hide* (2003), a novel, *She's Gone* (2007), a book of cultural criticism and theory, *Natural Mysticism*:

Towards A New Reggae Aesthetic (1999), and a personal narrative, *A Far Cry from Plymouth Rock* (2007).

Jean D'Costa (neé Creary) is best known as a writer of fiction for children. Her books include *Sprat Morrison* (1972), *Escape to Last Man Peak* (1976), *Voice in the Wind* (1978) and *Jenny and the General* (2006). She read English at the University College of the West Indies, did postgraduate work at Oxford, and was a member of the English Department at Mona from 1962 until 1977. Between 1977 and 1980 she was engaged in research into archaic Jamaican creole and culture, towards *Voices in Exile: Jamaican Texts of the 18th and 19th Centuries* (1989) and *Language in Exile: Three Hundred Years of Jamaican Creole* (1990), two volumes co-authored with Barbara Lalla. In 1980 she joined the faculty at Hamilton College, New York, retiring in 1998 as Leavenworth Professor Emeritus. She and her husband now live in Florida.

Honor Ford-Smith was artistic director of the Sistren Theatre Collective in Jamaica for many years. Her work with Sistren toured widely in Europe, North America and the Caribbean and earned several awards. She is co-author and editor of Sistren's collection of oral autobiographies, *Lionheart Gal: Lifestories of Jamaican Women* (1987), and author of a collection of poems, *My Mother's Last Dance* (1997). The play 'Fallen Angel and the Devil Concubine' which she co-created as a member of the Groundwork Company has been produced regionally and internationally. She has been Writer in Residence at the Oval Theatre in London and at Theatre Muraille in Toronto. She has worked as associate artistic director for Theatre Archipelago in Toronto and has had poetry broadcast on CBC radio. She is currently Assistant Professor of Community and Environmental Arts at York University in Toronto. Her PhD dissertation examined the pedagogy and politics of postcolonial Jamaican performance.

Rawle Gibbons was born in Belmont, Trindad. Between 1970 and 1984 he lived mostly in Jamaica, attending the University of the West Indies and teaching at the Jamaica School of Drama. He has done postgraduate work on the relation between folk forms and Caribbean theatre. He returned to Trinidad and in 1986 was appointed to the newly established Creative Arts Centre at St. Augustine. A playwright who is the author of *Shepherd* (1981), *I Lawah* (1984), *Ogun Iyan* (2006) and *A Calypso Trilogy* (1999), he is also known as an outstanding theatre director. Most of his recent productions have been collectively devised with his students at UWI.

Cecil Gray, who was born in 1923 in Port of Spain, Trinidad, now resides in Toronto. An actor and director in the first Trinidad theatre group, Whitehall Players, he also served as president of The Readers' and Writers' Guild. After earning a BSc (Econ) degree from the University of London in 1958, he did the Diploma in Education course at the University of the West Indies, Mona, and began lecturing in the School of Education in 1960. He produced several textbooks for secondary and primary schools, including *Bite In*, *Language for Living*, *English for Life*, and *Swing into English*. Director of the In-Service Diploma in Education Programme at UWI, Mona, and later at St. Augustine, he retired in 1983. Cecil Gray is also a poet, the author of six collections, including *The Woolgatherer* (1994), *Lillian's Songs* (1996), *Leaving the Dark* (1998) and *Plumed Palms* (2000).

Kendel Hippolyte, who was born in St. Lucia in 1952, studied at Mona in the 1970s, and has done postgraduate work on drama and society in St. Lucia. An actor and a director, he co-founded the Lighthouse Theatre Company which has mounted more than forty productions. He has written seven plays, including *Drum-Maker*, *The Song of One: The Journey of Ti-Marie*, and *Triptych*. He is the author of five books of poetry, including *Birthright* (1997) and *Night Vision* (2006). He has been the recipient of literary prizes in St. Lucia, a James Michener Fellowship to study poetry and an OAS scholarship to study theatre. He was awarded the St. Lucia Medal of Merit (Gold) in 2000 for his contribution to the arts.

Merle Hodge, a Trinidadian who is Senior Lecturer in the Faculty of Humanities and Education, UWI, St. Augustine campus, has taught at secondary and tertiary levels in different Caribbean countries. Her PhD thesis was on 'Earl Lovelace and the Evolution of Voice in the History of the Novel in Trinidad and Tobago'. She is a member of the Advisory Council to the Academy at the University of Trinidad and Tobago for Arts, Letters, Culture and Public Affairs, and a founding member of Women Working for Social Progress (Workingwomen). The author of two novels — *Crick Crack, Monkey* (1970) and *For the Life of Laetitia* (1993) — she has also published short stories, as well as several articles in local and international periodicals on Caribbean literature, language, family and gender issues.

Joan Andrea Hutchinson is a Jamaican writer-performer, co-author of at least two revues in which she also performed — *Children Children* and the award-winning *Laugh Jamaica*, which is available on video. She is the conceptualizer and producer/director of *Lawd Di Riddim* Sweet, a CD recording of Louise Bennett with a studio audience in Toronto. Joan Andrea's cassettes/CDs include *Jamaica Ridim & Ryme*, *Wild About Jamaica*, *Anancy & Aunty Joan*, and *Hamper of Jamaican Proverbs*. She is the author of the book *Meck Mi Tell Yuh* (2004), a selection of her poems and dramatic monologues. A UWI graduate currently pursuing a Masters in Communication, she has also studied in the Netherlands, South Korea, Japan, Benin, the United States and Mexico.

Paul Keens-Douglas is one of the most eloquent and best-known raconteurs and social commentators in the English-speaking Caribbean. Born in Trinidad, he spent his early childhood in Grenada, where he attended Presentation College. He studied commercial broadcasting and radio/TV production in New York, earned a degree in sociology at Sir George Williams University (Concordia) in Montreal, and did postgraduate work at UWI, Mona. He has released nine books (including *Tanti at De Oval* and *Savannah Ghost*), at least fifteen albums, three videos and many CDs. His work is featured in many international publications and has been translated into German and Japanese. A pioneer in the development of oral traditions and the use of the vernacular as a literary medium, he produces the annual carnival Talk Tent which he started in 1983. His company, Keensdee Productions Ltd, focuses on management and staff training, with an emphasis on interpersonal and cross-cultural communication.

Mark McWatt was born in Georgetown, Guyana, in 1947. He attended schools all over the country, including mission schools in interior districts, as his father was a district officer in the colonial government of the time. He studied at the University of Toronto and the University of Leeds. Since 1976 he has been on the staff of the University of the West Indies, Cave Hill campus, where he is Professor of West Indian Literature. He was founding editor of the *Journal of West Indian Literature* (*JWIL*). A poet, he is the author of *Interiors* (1989) and *The Language of Eldorado* (1994) which won the Guyana Prize. His collection of short stories, *Suspended Sentences: Fictions of Atonement* (2006), won three international literary prizes: the regional (Canada and the Caribbean) Commonwealth Writers' Prize for the best first book of fiction; the overall Commonwealth Writers' Prize for the best first book of fiction; and the Casa de las Americas prize for best book of Caribbean Literature in English or Creole.

Brother Resistance — born Roy Lewis in Port of Spain, Trinidad — is one of the founding elders of Rapso. The term Rapso was coined in 1980 when he and his Network Riddum Band released their debut album, *Busting Out*. Brother Resistance, also known as Lutalo Masimba, has gone on to become one of Trinidad's best known performers. He traces

Rapso out of the oral traditions of Africa, the griot who was spokesman for the community or the tribe, and through voluble Carnival figures such as the Chantuelle, the Pierrot Grenade and the Midnight Robber. He is the author of the book *Rapso Explosion*, and has made many recordings, including *Touch the Earth with Rapso* and *De Power of Resistance*. 'Rapso,' he has said, 'is more than an art form. It is really an attitude.... The colonial Jumbie is forever present.... Everything is like foreign impressions. Through Rapso we embrace an attitude that would help to fight against that sort of thing and to establish ourselves to the world.'

Olive Senior, who was born in Jamaica, now resides in Toronto. Her non-fiction works include the *Encyclopedia of Jamaican Heritage* (2003) and *Working Miracles: Women's Lives in the English-Speaking Caribbean* (1991). Her short-story collections are *Summer Lightning* (1986) which won the Commonwealth Writers' Prize, *Arrival of the Snake Woman* (1989) and *Discerner of Hearts* (1995). Her books of poetry are *Talking of Trees* (1986), *Gardening in the Tropics* (1994) and *Over the Roofs of the World* (2005) which was short-listed for Canada's Governor-General's Award for Literature. She has been editor of two of the Caribbean's leading journals, *Social and Economic Studies* and *Jamaica Journal*. She has received the Norman Washington Manley Award for Excellence, and the Musgrave Gold Medal from the Institute of Jamaica. She has been an Arts Council of England International Writer in Residence, a Hawthornden Fellow, and Writer in Residence at several universities.

Jean Small came to Jamaica in 1954 to study at the University College of the West Indies. Though she has also worked in Guyana, Trinidad, Nigeria, and Australia, most of her life as a professional educator has been spent in Jamaica. She has taught French in secondary schools and at university. Her publications include textbooks in French and Spanish. She is also an award-winning actress, director and playwright, author of *A Black Woman's Tale* and articles on the theatre of empowerment. She also uses theatre as a tool for teaching French Language and Literature. She has been honoured by the French Government for distinguished teaching of French. She led the team of Caribbean experts who formulated the CXC French curriculum and she helped to write the syllabus for CXC Theatre Arts.

Printed in the United States
85821LV00002B/169-552/A